CREATED FOR LOVE

*Reclaiming Jesus's Vision for
Sexuality, Gender & Relationships*

ANDREW FRANKLIN

CREATED FOR LOVE

Published by Clear Day Publishing, a division of Clear Day Media Group LLC, Waco, TX, cleardaypublishing.com.

Published in association with Lux Creative {theluxcreative.com}

ISBN: 978-1-7342917-0-4
Library of Congress Control Number: 2020925731

Cover Design: Carolynn Seibert
Interior Design: Lux Creative {theluxcreative.com}

Printed in the United States of America.

ENDORSEMENTS

"Created for Love is a welcome resource for all who seek clear under-standing regarding sexuality and Christianity. Andrew Franklin shares from his own journey and from his years of pastoring others who struggle with sexual identity. He gives practical ideas on how the church can have a biblical, yet loving response to the confusion of our day."
— **Gary Chapman, Ph.D.**, author of *The 5 Love Languages*

"One thing the world needs more of is people who are self-aware but others-focused. Andrew Franklin is a stand-out here; not just because of his radical life story but because he's not preaching a message; he's living one. If people knew Jesus the way that Andrew reveals Him in this book, they would ALL run to Him. Let the intimacy that Andrew has found with God reorient you, open up a deeper compassion for those who seem desperately beyond reach of God, and heal areas of your own heart. I wish everyone approached those identifying as LGBTQ this way."
— **Ken Williams**, pastor at *Bethel Church* (Redding, CA), founder of *CHANGED Movement*

"I am excited for you to not only read this book, but more importantly, to engage with the rich content and years of inner-healing and ministry experience that Andrew unpacks in these pages. Having known Andrew, and his wife Jordyn, for quite a few years and connecting with them in ministry contexts has been deeply enriching for me and my wife. I particularly value and also champion the overarching message of the more that God has for us and how powerful it is when fellow believers see that vision of God's *more* for one another. While struggle and pain are an inevitable part of our human journey and process of sanctification, hope, joy and peace are also traveling companions. Andrew blesses us with these realities throughout this important work."
— **Garry Ingraham**, director of *Love & Truth Network*

"As a pastor in Seattle, I've personally experienced the desperate need for church leaders and members to be crystal clear on Biblical World-view. But to actually help people who are struggling, our clarity must be backed by personal integrity and led with Jesus' love. *Created For Love* will help us get there!"

— **Andrew Bach**, lead pastor, *Mosaic Community Church*, Seattle WA

"I savored this book because it reflects the pedigree of its author and the One who set him free. Andrew Franklin combines profound biblical scholarship, a clear philosophy of what it means to be human (spirit housed in flesh), relevant psychological insights on becoming human, and a zesty spirituality that inspires and provokes us to become the man or woman Jesus summons from our sin-stalled state. Besides that, he quotes Graham Greene in between Adele and Flannery O'Connor! Who is this Franklin character? Simply put, a whip smart, humble father and husband whose journey out of homosexuality runs like a river through this straightforward guide to becoming a Christian in all aspects of one's life, including the sexual. And as a pastor who has majored in restoring adults hobbled by all manner of sexual brokenness, Franklin insists that wholeness can only be ours by taking our places as members of Christ in His healing community. Without trivializing our wounds, Franklin offers us a guide and a choice to resume the way of Jesus, with walking partners."

— **Andrew Comiskey**, founding director, *Desert Stream Ministries*

CONTENTS

ACKNOWLEDGMENTS

Years ago, I heard a theologian present a re-telling of the gospel of Mark. In the midst of his enthralling lecture, he stated something that has stuck with me. He said, in my paraphrase, "You don't have to be original when you're presenting truth, you just need to be correct." I am very aware that I have little to say that's original, and I certainly can't pretend to always be correct. I truly stand on the backs of men and women who have beautiful, powerful, in-depth material on the topics of gender, sexual ethics, healing and restoration. If reading this material does nothing else but introduce you to these gifts, I will be more than satisfied. My goal in developing this material was not to establish myself as a new authority, but rather to compile some core messages from these true authorities, to introduce their work to those who may not be aware of it, and to put together the theology, psychology, and good pastoral advice that has blessed my life.

In the world of understanding the Biblical witness regarding gender and sexuality, I am indebted to Brent Avery — his dissection of the first words of Genesis have had a lasting impact on my understanding of what it means to be human. On this foundation, much was built from the teachings and writings of Dr. Robert A. J. Gagnon, whose *The Bible and Homosexual Practice* cannot be bested for thorough scholarship and fearless, compassionate truth-telling. A few years later, I was introduced to the work of Christopher West in his creative presentation of the work of St. Pope John Paul II's *Theology of the Body*. Attending his week-long teaching of the material formed much of the basis of what is presented in the first half of this book. His books and teachings are joyful, true, and deep.

In understanding gender development and causes of gender insecurity, I grossly oversimplify the powerful work of Dr. Joseph Nicolosi, particularly his masterwork *Shame and Attachment Loss*. Those looking for deeper understanding of the roots of dissociation from a birth gender and sexual identity need look no further than this work.

Three people in particular have formed my philosophy and practice of pastoral care and counsel as one who seeks to bring healing and restoration to broken people. The first to impact me was Stephen Black. He directs a parachurch counseling ministry called First Stone Ministries and co-founded Restored Hope Network, a group of ministries with endless experience and expertise in the realm of helping people step into the gift of sexual integrity, purity, and clarity of the meaning of their bodies. Stephen introduced me first to the work of Leanne Payne, whose books (most notably *Crisis in Masculinity*, *Real Presence*, and *The Healing Presence*) have done much to form my view of pastoral care and the intersection of psychological and spiritual truth to bring healing to the soul.

Last, but most significant of all my influences, Andrew Comiskey has pioneered and paved the way to see the church become a place of clear, shining love, mercy and redemption for decades now. I am endlessly indebted to his influence through his writing, his leadership, and his personal mentorship. A case could very well be made that this book is nothing more than a condensed expression of his masterful guidebook *Living Waters: Restoring Relational Integrity Through the Broken Body of Christ*. In my opinion, he stands tall in this company of pillars in the church whose work is serving as salt to preserve us as we prepare to become one with Jesus.

A more complete bibliography can be found at the end of this book, but in case any of my readers are familiar with the aforementioned authors and protest that I am stealing ideas and concepts from authors more experienced and accomplished than myself, I wanted to be the first to wholeheartedly and joyfully agree.

In addition to personal influences, you'll find here many stories culled from the great work God has done in men and women alongside whom I've had the privilege to walk. They are friends, fellow church members, and Christ-followers in their own right. I've changed their names and some minor details of their stories to protect their privacy, but I'm so grateful for the community that has given me a larger perspective of Jesus's redemptive work than I'd ever have on my own. I am thankful for each of their lives and stories and for the permission to share them in this context.

This book is dedicated to the amazing people of Antioch Norman.
Thank you for championing Jordyn and me through so many seasons.
Thank you for opening your lives to us and to Jesus, that we might have the
privilege of seeing Him bring healing and deliverance in so many ways.
Thank you for your generosity that empowered both this book's content
and publication.
This is your story as much as mine.
Your love has forever marked us.

INTRODUCTION

In May 2006, I found myself spent. Done. I was 23 years old, a struggling actor in New York. I'd identified as gay for several years, initially feeling liberated in the ability to embrace and pursue my powerful sexual attractions. Sometimes that looked like party hook-ups or one-night stands. Sometimes that looked like a friendship I became obsessed with that eventually became sexual, romantic, or occasionally (but not often) both. Sometimes that looked like attempting a romance, only to end up more disillusioned, disappointed, and generally annoyed than ever before. As these experiences piled up, what also piled up was a sense of shame. Less and less could I find anything lovely within myself. More and more I felt untrustworthy. Dirty.

Growing up in a conservative Christian home, I had attempted to stuff down my sexual attractions, believing the proper response to sexual feelings was to annihilate them. "Take this away!" I would pray, only to feel frustrated at the silence from God. As a young adult, my attempt to embrace and find fulfillment of my longings on my own terms were equally futile — embracing my desires meant using other people to feel good, which made me a jerk. In other words, what I came to realize was, *I needed saving.*

In May 2006, Jesus did just that. A Cinco de Mayo party turned sour, as my drug and alcohol use led to a night I didn't remember. I came to find out I had abhorrently disrespected several friends and had sexually assaulted another man. My shame finally stared me in the face, and under its harsh gaze, I cried out to Jesus. I hit the ground and prayed the only thing I knew to pray at that point: "Okay Jesus, I'm done. I'm yours." I had no idea what that was supposed to mean for my sexuality or my body. I just knew I needed saving.

Jesus responded to me with such kindness. "I'm not mad at you," I heard in my heart, and somehow I knew it was Jesus — His way of speaking the truth of Scripture to me: "The one who comes to me I will never cast out."[1] That statement cut against the grain of everything I thought was correct but showed me a love that didn't end due to disappointment, fear, or offense. I had my first taste of a truly divine love.

That experience with love opened up a whole new way of loving and living. Initially, as with most new Christians, I needed a whole lot of help from skilled and mature believers. The goal wasn't a conversion from gay to straight — just a conversion from lust to learning the way of Jesus.

Jesus began to show me why I felt the way I felt, why I wanted the things I wanted, why I'd done the things I'd done. In the process, He gave me a whole new vision of Himself as my perfect Father and the source of the healing, restoration, and love I needed. As He showed me who He was, and surrounded me with Christians who were gracious to me in my mess and truthful to me in my confusion, I began to see myself as a man who didn't need the "gay" label to feel like I made sense, who didn't need sexual addiction to make me feel wanted. I became simply a man in the world of men, and a brother in the family of God.

My decision to follow Jesus came well over a decade ago. Over the course of the following years, Jesus has taken me on a journey to understanding my body, its purposes, and my capacity to give and receive love in ways that bring life and order, not harm and confusion, to the earth. As I experienced the joy of restoration, I slowly began to reach out to others to offer some of the words of healing and hope that had given life to me.

In my years of ministry, I've seen Jesus respond in extravagant mercy, and I've seen many men and women who have unique stories but common needs for healing and restoration. We really aren't such confusing messes when seen in the light of God's loving wisdom.

Five years into my life with Jesus, I met a woman named Jordyn and became friends with her through my church. After gaining some foundations in what love looks like from Jesus and healthy friends, I gradually found myself able to offer myself to this woman — first as a friend, eventually as a husband. Through all this, Jesus has met me again and again to show me the difference between love *Andrew's* way

---

[1] John 6:37 (All Scripture references are English Standard Version (ESV), unless otherwise noted)

and love *Jesus's* way. Loving Jordyn, receiving her love, and allowing Jesus to love her through me has been the joy of my life and my most consistent window into the heart of God.

We haven't arrived — we consistently find ourselves apologizing, hurting, and crying out for mercy from God and each other — but our lives with one another and our children have been the best of classrooms to learn about holy love in the midst of a broken humanity.

Moreover, I've seen the power of God express itself through the many men and women I've been able to walk with who have similarly needed a transformation of the way they've looked at their bodies, sexuality, and hunger for love. I've seen Jesus raise them up to be the most authentic witnesses to love and redemption that I know. Truly, He uses the weak and foolish people of this world to shame the wise.[2]

In finding the purpose of our bodies, gender, and sexuality, I believe we catch a glimpse, albeit a very tiny one, of the heart of God and the heart of the gospel. In the process of healing and transformation Jesus offers us, we not only see His beauty, we also become truly beautiful ourselves — powerful expressions of the God who loves extravagantly, who *is* love. Because God created us in His image, He is uniquely qualified to define how we love. Because Jesus took on flesh, He is uniquely qualified to redeem us. Because Holy Spirit has been poured out on humanity, He is capable of filling us with love that is full, free, passionate, and pure.

THE UNIVERSAL STORY

There's a hunger in each of our hearts — a hunger to experience more than we have yet known. That hunger for "more" can lead us in many directions — to seek more food, more money, more power — and that hunger has led to the highest highs and lowest lows in humanity's existence and in each of our lives as well.[3] Most of you reading this book could probably tell me about a time in your life you sought something you desperately wanted, and you'd either grin as you shared the fulfillment of that hunger, or you'd get uncomfortable and shifty-eyed as you

---

[2] 1 Corinthians 1:27
[3] Christopher West writes at length on the concept of relational hunger, particularly in his book *Fill These Hearts.*

told me that you either didn't get what you wanted, or you did — and it wasn't pretty.

This insatiable human appetite is written all over our cultural touchstones, and the crux of the hunger — whatever first appearances would tell us — always seems to point to the ultimate hunger: love. In her enormously successful single "Rolling in the Deep," pop icon Adele lamented "We could have had it *all*," and we have all resonated with the hope of a love that could give us everything, and the disappointment we have experienced from people who gave us less than *all*.

All over the world we have heard about options available for the filling of this desire for intimacy, and we've heard the bitter disappointment that comes when people didn't get it or did get it but it wasn't pretty. Some of the best-selling music of all time revolves around the break-up album — we buy it because we find comfort in knowing someone else has experienced the disappointment of a love promised and then withheld.

We've also responded to the celebratory, even crazed, music and art stemming from the hope or excitement of love within our grasp. We respond to movies and music that seems to express the fulfillment of all the longings of the heart, but somewhere we're cynical that the relationships our heroes pursue are really going to pan out. So, we vacillate between the getting-laid dance pop and the break-up anthem.

We find another of our world's options for meeting the hunger — filling it vicariously through a virtual world, a world full of cheap intimacy, but intimacy easily experienced. Pornography is the highest-selling industry in the world, making a killing off trafficked men and women who, sometimes willingly but usually under compulsion, participate in a thrilling, cheap, fake experience of intimacy with strangers around the world. Many who don't participate in graphic pornography are happy consumers of imagined characters filling the world's best-selling book genre (by a wide margin) — romance & erotica literature. Quite literally, our cultural images and imagination are consumed with sex, while rejecting the notion of a spiritual fulfillment for this desire.

CHURCH AND THE HUNGER

Many churches claim to have found the answer to our desire for love that never fails. Often, we have heard their message: Jesus Himself is an expression of love from God, forgiving our sins and personifying a love that will go the distance for us. Spiritually, a way is made for us to know, receive, and give love, but what about our physical hunger for intimacy? Does Jesus have anything to offer us there?

To this realm, our church experiences have often been quite disappointing, haven't they? Misinterpretation of Biblical exhortations to crucify the flesh has led many to believe that their bodies are suspicious, dirty, or inherently evil. Relegating holy intimacy to something that is exclusively spiritual leaves exactly one-half of our human nature without any sense of purpose or understanding. On the other hand, current church trends point Christians to forget the weight of spiritual ethics and embrace whatever sexual or gender expressions are culturally *en vogue*. Love is love is love, they tell us. But we are body and spirit, and those Christians who have been able to transcend worldly satisfaction and find the desires of their bodies and their souls fulfilled in Jesus have become something beyond morally upright. They've become mystics. Saints[4].

My prayer for this book is to capture a small glimpse of God's heart in creating our bodies *and* our spirits to work in tandem. I want Jesus's Church to have the courage to gaze into the powerful reality of our bodies and see them, not lustfully, but through the eyes of God. This is tough work, but the alternatives are to continue seeing human nature either lustfully or suspiciously, and I'm not satisfied with those alternatives. I hope those of you holding this book aren't satisfied with those options either. I bet you aren't. Because if we listen to the Spirit's urging in our hearts, we can hear the Divine heartbeat: "I earnestly desire that they also, whom you have given me, may be with me where I am" (John 17:24). Longing. Intimacy. Relationship. God. Man. Flesh. Spirit. All in unity, all working in tandem to express the very heart of God.

THE MESSAGE OF THE GOSPEL

For the last half century, Satan has been mostly winning a war aimed at the very heart of the gospel: the human body and its capacity to show forth the beauty, glory, love and power of God. To believe in Jesus is to believe that God can be shown forth through a human body

---

[4] Christopher West, *Theology of the Body Explained*, p. 599-600

and that God's love can become reality through the way a human body offers and longs for intimacy. Sexual perversion, gender confusion, and assault on vulnerable human life has all centered around who crafts the human body and who dictates what it's used for. In a world where almost everybody would champion love, few have stopped to question what love looks like, and if the powerful force motivating us is truly love at all or something quite different. May we all be given eyes that see and ears that hear just what God has created us for:

"What is man, that you are mindful of him?" (Psalm 8:4)

PART ONE

The

Biblical

Witness

Chapter One

WHAT WE WERE
MADE FOR

"In the image of God He made them, male and female
He created them."
Genesis 1:27

Before we understand how Jesus restores our sexuality, we need to take a step back to the beginning. How were we made and what were we made for? This is a very important question, because finding God's intentions in creating us gives us an essential glimpse into where He's taking us in the process of redemption. "Restoration" and "redemption" are words that imply a return to origin. God's created intention is for us to reveal His power and personality through the dynamic unity of male and female.

If we go to the creation account, we see God hovering, contemplating: "The Spirit of God was brooding over the waters of the deep" (Genesis 1:2). There was potential untapped. Day by day, we see things gradually build with a kind of rhythm, a progression to greater and greater things, like a symphony, crescendoing as instruments are added.

Light, darkness.

Evening, morning.

Heaven.

Evening, morning.

Earth, water, plants.

Evening, morning.

Sun, moon, stars.

Evening, morning.

The crescendo continues and builds.

Fish, birds, sea monsters — the first creatures that can reproduce. God blesses their ability to reproduce their own lives and commissions them to do so.

Evening, morning.

Cattle, creeping things. beasts.

Then, finally, the crowning achievement, the swell in the music. This is the first time that Scripture breaks from prose into poetic meter. I think of it as similar to the way a Broadway musical transitions from dialogue into song and dance — mere words aren't enough to convey the emotion and passion at play.

"Then God said, 'Let us make man in Our image, according to Our likeness; and let them rule over the fish of the sea and over the birds of the sky and over the cattle and over all the earth, and over every creeping thing that creeps on the earth.'

So God created man in His own image, in the image of God He created him; male and female He created them" (Genesis 1:26-27).

This poetry sung by God tells us a few things about what it means to be human:

1. **We were created to look like the invisible God.** The blueprint for our bodies is somehow found within God, and the blueprint for our souls somehow is also fashioned after the spirit of God. As a great theologian has said, "The body, and it alone, is capable of making visible what is invisible, the spiritual and divine. It was created to transfer into the visible reality of the world, the invisible mystery hidden in God from time immemorial, and thus to be a sign of it."[5]

---

[5] John Paul II, *Man and Woman He Created Them: A Theology of the Body* (TOB), Feb 20, 1980.

2. **Our gender as male and female is connected to exhibiting God's image.** His image includes both masculinity and femininity and he creates male and female to exhibit the fullness of His image and character.

Every other created being was good, displayed beauty, even displayed unique characteristics. But only our humanity was given special favor and deemed "very good" (Gen. 1:31). Our gendered humanity alone is stamped with the look of God.

CREATED WITH BODIES

Let's look again at Genesis 2:7: "Then the Lord God formed man of dust from the ground and breathed into his nostrils the breath of life; and man became a living being."

God formed our bodies, which give us form and structure, from the earth. He supplied our breath, or life, from Himself. We were designed to be at home and at peace in our male and female bodies and also designed to be filled with Spirit that can only come from God.

In Hebrew Scripture and thought, the Holy Spirit is literally "Ruach HaKodesh" — the Holy Breath or Wind. This is why, in Acts 2, the writers point out the importance of the wind that was present as a mark of the Holy Spirit in the midst of the people of God.[6] So, while we can recognize that we all need physical breath to live, God is also expressing here the importance of both a physical, embodied humanity and a spirit-filled, God-breathed inspiration in order to fulfill our human calling and potential.

Only when body and spirit are active and united with Holy Spirit is man fully alive. This perspective gives new enlightenment to the lie of Satan spoken in Genesis 3, when he told Eve she wouldn't really die if she ate the forbidden fruit.[7] From a physical perspective, Adam and Eve didn't die, at least immediately, when they ate the forbidden fruit. Although I believe that physical death was never part of our intended existence, and this physical death did enter in through Adam's sin,

---

[6] Acts 2:2
[7] Genesis 3:4

this death exists because of the death of the spiritual, inner life that occurred immediately when Adam and Eve sinned. After eating the fruit, although Adam and Eve kept their bodies and their physical breath, their unity with Holy Spirit, which had led to their nakedness without shame, was cut off by their sin. Thus, although physically alive, they ceased to fulfill their human potential and began hiding. *The body severed from the life and inspiration of Holy Spirit is unable to reach its destiny as a human being.*

While our bodies are incomplete without a spiritual life, the inverse of this is also true. Our spiritual life, when separated from our practical, physical, sensory life, has no form and cannot function. Rather, God has created us to "incarnate" — to put flesh on the spiritual life by living out our faith in our bodies.[8] As Paul would state thousands of years later, "I have been crucified with Christ, and it is no longer I who live. Jesus Christ now lives in me."[9]

CREATED WITH DESIRE

In the second creation account, found in Genesis 2, we get another dimension to the story: "Then the Lord God formed man of dust from the ground and breathed into his nostrils the breath of life; and man became a living being" (Genesis 2:7).

The word in this scripture translated as "being" (NASB) or "soul" (ESV) is fascinating. The Hebrew word is "nephesh", and it occurs over 750 times in the Old Testament alone.[10] Mostly, it's translated with the words above. However, there is another translation of "nephesh," that refers to being alive. That word is "appetite."

"All the work of a man is for his mouth, yet his appetite [nephesh] is not filled" (Ecclesiastes 6:7).

A few other places, 'nephesh" is translated as "desire":

"Better what the eyes see than the wandering of desire [nephesh]" (Ecclesiastes 6:9).

A biblical dimension of being human - made to be like God - is having desire, appetites, and longings. This is what it means to be alive.

---

[8] West, *Theology of the Body Explained*, p. 14.

[9] Galatians 2:20

[10] On the meanings of the Hebrew "nephesh," I pull from the unpublished teachings of Brent Avery.

And if, as we know to be true, God's ultimate longing is for relationship, we can bless *our* relational longings, *our* longings for intimacy, and see that, even though they may often be misdirected and perverted, the desire for intimacy itself is an expression not of perversion, but of our godly image.

This has very important implications for our sexuality. All too often, we can buy into a very tricky lie: sexual desire is inherently bad, and holiness equals killing our desires for intimacy. From God's perspective, being appetite-free means being dead. In God's sovereign wisdom, our desires need not be killed but rather directed and satisfied in the right ways.

There's another place we see this theme of "nephesh". It relates to souls that are alive to and consumed by desire. The Hebrew prophet and apostle John receives revelation of the very throneroom and dwelling place of God. Around the person of God, he sees living creatures, circling Jesus day and night, never having enough of His presence. They are always crying out "Holy! Holy! Holy!" — continually in awe of the presence and personality of Jesus.[11] These creatures find the desires of their heart not annihilated, but heightened and satisfied in a continuous cycle of pursuit and rapture as they experience new dimensions of their Creator and King.

Desire as evil? Nonsense! Desires are made not to be squelched but to be eternally satiated.

THE REJECTION AND REDEMPTION OF THE BODY

Hatred of the body affected me deeply as a young Christian struggling with long-standing sexual struggles. I vividly remember a period of time shortly after I decided to follow Jesus. I felt a deep desire for holiness but an equally deep hopelessness that I could ever achieve sexual purity. Sexual addiction had been all I'd known for years. I felt enslaved to lust. It seemed clear to me that the best path would be emasculation — surgical castration. In my despair, I thought about Jesus's words, that it would be better for me to lose an eye than to go to hell, and I thought that maybe the holiest thing I could do would be to mar and reject my body in order to live a truly Christian life.

---

[11] Revelation 4:8

I never actually pursued this plan. Mercifully, Jesus led the way for me to get what I really needed, which was counseling. Far from wanting me to butcher my body, Jesus re-directed me into the much longer, more difficult work of reconciling my heart to my body and taking authority over the body He'd given me. Instead of affirming my body hatred, this counselor exhorted me to live out Paul's command to "present the members of your body as instruments of righteousness."[12] As I blessed my body parts and affirmed their purpose as a way to reveal God - especially the body parts that had been stumbling blocks for me - I began to see my body as a powerful substance to be treated with dignity rather than perversion.

In the years since that crisis I've encountered many Christians who seem to think that victory would look like never having to experience or navigate a sexual desire. These Christians live in a state of impotent spirituality and perpetual defeat. Peace and joy come when we are able to both receive God's blessing over our sexual bodies and rejoice in the long and hard work of learning to appropriately direct our desires and bodily longings.

The unification of body and spirit is at the very heart of why God created human beings. Think about it: God had already created beings that had spirits without bodies. They're called *angels*. And God had already created physical bodies without an infusion of Holy Spirit. They're called *animals*.[13] Remember: the body alone makes visible what is invisible: spiritual and divine truths.

While there is admittedly a great danger in living the physical life cut off from the spirit, I also believe there's a great danger for spiritual people — including Christians — who seek to live the life of the spirit cut off from the life of the body. Just like Satan did while tempting Jesus in the wilderness in Matthew 4, we can even use Scripture to back up our faulty beliefs about the body.

The apostle Paul wrote, "For to set the mind on the flesh is death, but to set the mind on the spirit is life and peace. For the mind that is set on the flesh is hostile to God, for it does not submit to God's law; indeed, it cannot" (Romans 8:6-7). How many of us have read his words

---

[12] Romans 6:13
[13] Christopher West, TOB Explained, p. 39

and been tempted to believe that the physical life is our problem, and our solution is to disembody ourselves in order to live in the spirit? I believe Satan has a lot invested in getting Christians to believe in this self-hating view of our bodies. After all, a body is one thing that Satan doesn't have (more on this later).

If Paul's not telling us to think negatively about our bodies or our physical humanity, what is he telling us? Throughout Paul's writings, he emphasizes the importance of living by the spirit, in opposition to living in light of fleshly desires. What's more, a main theme of the New Testament is a resurrection of the life of the spirit. Jesus' resurrection marks the first time period in human history since Adam's fall when we can live in unity with the Spirit of God. This is the Good News! For thousands of years before Jesus imparted Holy Spirit to us, all humanity had known was a life revolving around the body and its desires, *as severed and separated from the life and inspiration of God*. This division is the life set around the flesh rather than the spirit. To contrast this divided life, Paul presents the good news: we have an ability, through Jesus, to live *in* our bodies, motivated and moved *by* our spirit, and can overcome the divisions that lead to death.

"And they that are Christ's have crucified the flesh with its lusts and desires. If we live by the Spirit, let us also keep in step with the spirit" (Galatians 5:24-25).

As Christians, our bodies aren't being crucified unto death. Rather, our lustful inclination to live in opposition to the spirit is being crucified, so that our bodies can "keep in step" with the Spirit — not getting ahead of God or lagging behind in disobedience but living out our physical humanity in a unity and partnership with Holy Spirit. *This* is what we were made for.

CREATED WITH GENDER

Another aspect of the creation account gives us an important glimpse into the purpose of our bodies and the way we were created to embody and image God. It's the duality of gender. "In the image of God He made them male and female" (Genesis 1:27).

Throughout the ages, Judeo-Christian theologians have gazed into the mystery of a God who is singular and plural at the same time. Hebrew scholars grapple with a God who declares "Let US make man in our image"; a God whose greatest commandment is itself an anomaly.

In the Hebrew language, just like in English, there are singular and plural nouns. There's me and there's we. In English, we can easily spot plural nouns because they usually end in "s" or "es". "God" means one God, "gods" means multiple gods. In Hebrew, we can easily spot plural nouns because they end in "im". "Eloi" means God, "Elohim" means gods. With that in mind, read what Jewish theologians call the Great Shema, the great commandment: "Hear, O Israel! The Lord our God [Elohim], The Lord [Elohim] is One!" In other words, the multiple God is One, seamlessly united.

The Catholic Church has put it this way: "But St. John goes even further when he affirms that "God is love": God's very being is love. By sending his only Son and the Spirit of Love in the fullness of time, God has revealed his innermost secret: God himself is an eternal exchange of love, Father, Son and Holy Spirit, and he has destined us to share in that exchange."[14]

In other words, how a plural God exists as one is simple: love. To go further, the exchange of love is what has brought new life and redemption, into the earth. In love, different entities become One and produce a world full of life.

This might still seem mysterious (and, in all honesty, it is), but we have a great help in that our gendered bodies are stamped with this truth. We all exhibit a specific kind of body, but share humanity with others who have a different, specific kind of body. Only when the two distinct entities of male and female achieve a unity, through an exchange of love, does new life come into the earth.

God has three distinct essences — Father, Son, and Holy Spirit. He has created our human bodies with distinct essences as well: male and female. Just as the union of the Father's will and the Son's will at the crucifixion brought forth the life of Holy Spirit into the children of God, so the union of a man's initiation and a woman's response to his love brings forth the new life of a baby.[15]

Think about it. If all you knew of God was the Father, you wouldn't see the full picture of God. If you only knew Jesus but rejected the Holy

---

[14] Catechism of the Catholic Church, 221

Spirit, you'd only catch one side of who God is. Likewise, if all we know is our own gender, or all we consider is a neutered humanity, cut off from revelation of gender, we'll only catch a part of what God is like. He exhibits His nature through both genders as we unite together in love.

MAN'S SPIRITUAL AND PHYSICAL ESSENCE

A man's body is angular. His sexual organs are created to be aimed in one direction, and from there springs the seeds of life. A man is fertile for his entire lifespan and actualizes that fertility in his moments of greatest pleasure and enjoyment. A man's body enters a dark and life-less space. As He expresses love in that dark space, that space becomes a place where life can flourish.

A man's spirit longs for the same things. Men were created to go into dark and lifeless areas of the world and bring a powerful sense of love and enjoyment that transforms lifeless areas into fruitful gardens. We thrive when pursuing and initiating change. In this way, men image the character of God as he lovingly pursues our dark, formless hearts and plants His seed of life that calls us into a lifelong covenant under His leadership.

God created man from dust, revealing a natural tendency of the man to relate to the earth in the realm of tasks. When man was created, he first saw his creator, the God who is above him in authority and lead-ership. He was then given a commission to name the animals,[16] who are lower and made to submit to his leadership and will be defined by his evaluation. Man is created to see order and to call things into their proper place in the order of creation.

WOMAN'S SPIRITUAL AND PHYSICAL ESSENCE

A woman's body is supple. Her sexual organs are created to be open, receptive, and able to house new life and fully nurture it. A woman is fertile quite rarely but can create new life when feeling great pleasure or great pain. Sometimes she senses both simultaneously. A woman's body receives someone outside of herself and receives him into her most vulnerable places. As she accepts him in this intimate way, she

---

[15] This conceptual metaphor is taken from Christopher West's teaching of *Theology of the Body.*
[16] Genesis 2:19

becomes a house for a life that will outlive and outlast herself. For a span of time, that life is completely housed and nurtured in a hidden way, within her very body. After her baby is born, her body produces nourishment through the time of that life's greatest vulnerability, until the time her child is able to sustain itself.

A woman's spirit longs for the same things. Women's hearts were made to take in stimuli on multiple levels, in a constant way. They are living receptors. Intuition operates powerfully in women, who can have an innate hunch about the essence of things, contrasting the logical, linear knowledge a man displays. Women were created to provide a sense of nurture and protection for the vulnerable. Women tend to display a gift for accepting and receiving people — whether it be into their homes or into a party or a work environment. They thrive at receiving and responding with their entire being. In this way, women model part of what it means to be human — created to respond to God's loving initiative, to completely receive His love in such a way that it takes form inside of us, eventually overtaking us with a new life that is completely contained within us but overflows out of us.

God created woman not from dust, but from man. This reveals a tendency in women to relate. When woman is created, she first sees man — her equal. Where man is wired to see order, woman is wired to see and seek synthesis — the equal importance and dignity of all of God's creatures. Order and clarity mean less to her than relationship and connection. Eve's desire is to come alongside and impart love rather than assert power.

THE DANCE OF MASCULINITY AND FEMININITY

Recognizing gender differences should by no means make us feel limited, but rather help us make sense of our distinct bodily and physical essence. Every human bears the image of God and also embodies humanity. Therefore, women are called to initiate change and impart life, just as men are called to receive the love and leadership of God. As we relate to one another, however, we find our genders expressing themselves in distinct ways.

When men are secure in their masculinity, they will quite naturally respond to challenge. Something within him will come alive when presented with the right adventure, the right problem to solve. When women are secure in femininity, they will quite naturally respond to relationship. Something within her will come alive when presented with a person in need of nurture, care, home.

What's more, men and women are most fully distinct as they give themselves to one another. We become fully human, not when we arrive at perfect theology, but "in the moment of communion" with the other gender.[17] As a man initiates love with his bride, he gives her the gift of his body, imparting it to her. Her openness to his love, her response to his gift, becomes itself a gift to him that he receives into himself. In this way, we catch a glimpse of the way Jesus fully gives Himself to the Bride taken out of His side, and as we give ourselves to Him, we are able to bring Him pleasure through our response and become a gift back to the Ultimate Giver.

God Himself is an eternal exchange of Love. The good news we carry is that God has invited us into this exchange, to live in a never-ending response to His perfect love and Spirit.

It is this whole-hearted reciprocity of love, in which each party has a distinctive and irreplaceable role, that has the capacity to bring forth life. Two initiators cannot create life without the home of a womb, nor is response fruitful without an external gift of life to be received. When everything is working in tandem, the dance of masculinity and femininity revealed in marriage gives us a powerful glimpse into the eternal dance of God as He offers love to us and awakens a whole-hearted response of love from us in return, bringing the beauty and challenge of new life continuously to the earth. We see in redemption the reclamation of God's first intention for us as humans: to reveal His power and personality through the dynamic unity of man and woman, bringing dignity and honor to both.

[17] John Paul II, *TOB*, 9:3.

Chapter Two

EAST OF EDEN

Soon after I came on staff as the Counseling Pastor at my church, I reconnected with a young man named Wesley who had just stepped down as a small group leader due to moral failure. I heard Wesley's all-too-common story: he was a charismatic young adult, leading others to worship God in church, but seeking alcohol and casual sex with women to feel worshipped at bars when no one was looking.

As he did the good, hard work of coming into the light and entering a process of restoration, he remained discouraged. One night I vividly remember him sharing a concern: After developing such an ingrained lifestyle of misusing women, how could he ever hope to have a marriage? As he gave vent to his hopelessness, deep grief flowed out of him, and a deep well of compassion met him from the men in our support group.

Two years later, as I officiated his wedding to a beautiful young woman in our church, I remembered Wesley's vulnerability and marveled at the redemption of God. Jesus has a way of transforming our disillusionment about love and marriage, making those who seem the most disqualified become shining lights of the hope and joy we were created for.

While the dance of man and woman - of God and humanity - is powerful and beautiful, why is it so hard to see it that way? In order to fully understand the world we live in, we must understand not only the original purposes of God that are moving forward in the work of restoration, but also the reality of our fall into sin. With the fall of Adam and Eve, we have inherited a distorted and shame-based view of our gendered humanity. After Genesis 1-2 and its poetic description of

Creation, we must unpack Genesis 3 — the reality of the curse upon all of humanity and its implications for us as a people participating in both brokenness and redemption.

Let's take a brief look again at life before the curse. Adam and Eve were naked and unashamed. They could see the glory of God revealed in themselves and in each other. We can imagine they experienced two things:

1. **They could *see* each other without of judgment, expectation, or disappointment.** When Adam looked at Eve, he could behold the beauty and glory of God through her body and her spirit which animated it. When Eve looked at Adam, she could behold the power and strength of God through his body and his spirit which animated it.

2. **They could be *seen* by the other without experiencing fear or shame.** Being fully seen by the other wasn't an occasion for fear but rather an experience of full, unconditional acceptance. Adam and Eve were seen nude, but without an ounce of fear of being judged, mistreated, rejected or used. This is what was normal for Adam and Eve; in fact, it was all they knew before their fall into sin.

It's important to note that we can only imagine this experience of nakedness with no presence of shame and describe it in the language of the **absence** of our "normal" experiences with men and women.[18] Even the writer of Genesis can only describe that the man and woman were both naked and did **not** feel shame. If they didn't feel shame, what did they feel? Living in a world where the fall is evident all around us, it can be hard to imagine the experiences of the original man and woman who had never experienced rejection, judgment, or shame. All they knew was acceptance, joy and peace — the whole-hearted giving and joyful receiving of love as they expressed it to one another. In fully knowing their Creator, they were also able to see, with unveiled faces, the eternal exchange of love, joy, and acceptance between Father, Son, Holy Spirit, and humanity.

Then…it happened.

---

[18] John Paul II, *TOB*, 16:4.

PARADISE LOST

"Now the serpent was more crafty than any other beast of the field that the Lord God had made. He said to the woman, 'Did God actually say, 'You shall not eat of any tree in the garden?'" (Genesis 3:1).

It's important to take note of what actually happened in this original breaking of trust between man, woman, and God, because the enemy works in the same way now as he did in the Garden of Eden.

First, Satan plants doubt in the couple's heart toward what God said to them.

"Did God actually say, 'You shall not eat of any tree in the garden? ...you will not surely die'"(Genesis 3:1b, 4a).

Any time we experience questions in ourselves that have this ring to them, we must take notice. We must recognize the voice of an intruder when we hear thoughts such as, "Did God actually command that? Was that ever really such a big deal? Maybe it used to be, but is it now? Did God actually say...?"

Secondly, Satan plants doubt in the couple's heart toward the very character of God.

"You will not surely die. For God knows that when you eat of [the forbidden fruit] your eyes will be opened, and you will be like God, knowing good and evil" (Genesis 3:4).

In other words, Satan gives us this message: God is threatened by you and is trying to control you and limit your life — your experiences and enjoyment of freedom. Test it. See whether obeying God (and his command that is questionable) is really *that* big a deal. Maybe your life will actually be better going your own way. Who's to say? Maybe God is withholding something really good and beneficial for you.

Often, we can see in our bodily desires an underlying theme along these lines. If a behavior or relationship could potentially feel good and possibly benefit all parties involved, why would God prohibit us from experiencing this pleasure?

Third, the woman (and the man who was evidently with her) noticed a truth — the forbidden fruit looked good! It was beautiful — "a delight to the eyes...desired to make one wise" (Gen. 3:6). This truth was evident all along, but now they notice the tree and its fruit through the lens of doubt and distrust rather than faith. When we see a truth through the lens of distrust in the character, generosity, and sufficiency of God, the truth becomes distorted. In a sense, the truth becomes a lie, because it is filtered through distrust and unbelief.[19]

THE EFFECTS OF THE FALL – SHAME

The first experience of the body under sin is shame. In Genesis 3, shame is described as an awareness of the man and woman's nakedness — an awareness that brings a desire to hide. Being seen is no longer safe and must be guarded against. Hiding feels better, safer.

Adam and Eve were never commanded not to be naked. Their bodies were blessed along with the entirety of their personhoods. They were commanded not to eat the fruit of one forbidden tree. Under the effects of sin, they didn't feel ashamed of their behavior, but felt ashamed instead of their bodies.

THE BODY AS A SOURCE OF SHAME

Why are our bodies the target of shame?

Earlier, we dissected what sets humans apart from animals and angels. Only in the human body does the spiritual take on a physical form. Our highest capacity as bodily creatures lies in the ability to exhibit spiritual truth through our physical being. The fulfillment of this potential is seen in the way Jesus's life in the flesh reveals the love of God to all of humanity.

Before Satan fell from grace, he was an angel — an angel of unusual talent, beauty and favor. He seems to have had it all.[20] Except for one thing. *Satan never had a body.* As an angelic being, Satan existed only as a spiritual creature. It seems, from Genesis 3, that he could take on an appearance of physical form, but that appearance was a snake's body, not that of a human.

It was jealousy towards God's power that brought about Satan's fall. When Satan chose to distrust God's character, jealousy entered in, as it does to all of us. When we are jealous, we desire to see another person's gifts destroyed and tarnished. So, if Satan succeeds in one thing, what does he want to see tarnished and ruined in us? It must be our bodies and their spiritual capabilities when united with the Holy Spirit. If Satan can ruin man's exhibition of truth through his body's union with

---

[19] James 3:14
[20] Isaiah 14:12-17

his spirit, man has become impotent in regard to Satan — has become lower rather than exalted above him. Satan desires to make man like the animals by separating his body and spirit.

When Adam and Eve align with Satan in the garden, they immediately experience their demise through a hatred of their naked bodies. Their bodies no longer are objects of joy and acceptance but must be hidden to be safe.

Our bodies are the very temple and dwelling place of the Holy Spirit.[21] They are designed to be consumed with the fire and passion of God — not shut-down or shame-filled but glorious and radiant. When we, like Adam and Eve, align ourselves with sin, we "act out" — we literally act outside of this fellowship of Holy Spirit and the design and desire of God to be with us in committed, eternal communion and passion.

MAN AND THE CURSE

The heart-shift from faith to distrust always precedes our behavior and is the unseen essence of the fall into sin. For Adam, this heart-shift manifests itself before he ever acts out in eating the fruit. For he had been called to initiate, to protect, to name and identify and maintain a clarity over what the created world was about.[22]

Before he ever ate the fruit, Adam was "with [Eve]" through the course of her dialogue with the enemy.[23] He must have seen two things: the fruit was not meant for eating, for God had expressly set it apart. And woman was not meant to ingest the fruit. She was never called to make herself like God through effort because she already had a way to be like God — through relationship. But Adam kept silent. In distrust, he became passive rather than proactive, thus displaying the first symptom of fallen man. Rather than confidently asserting his authority over the created order, he became fearful and silent regarding the distortion of creation for wrong purposes.

This reversal of authority is seen in man's immediate response when lovingly questioned by God about his behavior. God gently asks if

---

[21] 1 Corinthians 6:19
[22] For more on the curses of Genesis 3, and their effects on men and women, see Andrew Comiskey, *Strength in Weakness*, Chapter 2
[23] Genesis 3:6

man ate the fruit, and man *blames*: "The woman whom you gave to be with me, she gave me fruit of the tree, and I ate" (Genesis 3:12). In other words, maybe I did mess up, but only because of *her*.

MAN'S CURSE TODAY

I've seen blame replace authority so many times, and in so many ways, among men. It comes out in hundreds of different expressions and statements, but the heart of the message sounds something like this: "I'd be doing better in my life if *she* was in a better place, if *she* let me." Never mind the fact that man was created to lead woman into a place of health. Blame has replaced authority.

God highlights a few more changes in man's relationships due to this shift from faith to distrust, all with this theme: that over which man was created to have authority, now has authority over him. Look at it:

"Cursed is the ground because of you; in pain you shall eat of it all the days of your life; thorns and thistles it shall bring forth for you; and you shall eat the plants of the field. By the sweat of your face you shall eat bread, till you return to the ground, for out of it you were taken; for you are dust, and to dust you shall return" (Gen. 3:17-19).

Man, under the curse, suffers from workaholism and from a despair in his purpose and effectiveness. He becomes obsessed with productivity and fruitfulness from his work, while seeing less and less return for his increasing effort.

For me, the curse looked like a rejection of masculinity and the relationship with woman altogether. I found men in my life were either passive and dominated by women, or cocky and arrogant bullies, and I wanted no part in either of these destinies. Without ever having language for what I was doing (Satan loves to keep us in the dark about the motives of our hearts), I began to adopt feminine characteristics and tended to desire close friendship with women more than men. Thus, rather than taking authority over my own feelings and fighting for my masculinity, I participated in Adam's abdication of authority and allowed myself to slide into an unholy, enmeshed relationship with femininity — imitating her and becoming a caricature of her personality rather than a powerful counterpart to provide protection and leadership. Soon, created fantasies had authority over my mind, and I became powerless over lust and the oppressive belief that I was different from "normal" men.

For other men, the curse can take on myriad manifestations. When we shift away from faith into a distrust of God, we can become passive, tyrannical, angry, addicted, immature, obsessed with success, obsessed with sex, obsessed with games. Our gifting to *do, work, and name* all too easily becomes a liability rooted in workaholism and judging, bullying, or name-calling.

WOMAN AND THE CURSE

Scripture makes clear that Eve was deceived by the serpent,[24] unlike Adam who knowingly bought into brokenness. Rather than willfully abnegating her authority, she actually believed eating the fruit would turn out okay. Ever since, women have been harassed by the enemy's desire to see them believe lies about themselves, God and man.

As a result of her deception, one of woman's core callings — bearing God's image through childbearing and nurture — becomes an object of pain and difficulty rather than joy: "I will make your pains in childbearing severe — in pain you shall bring forth children".[25] Unlike life in the garden, new birth in a fallen world means pain, something dreaded rather than desired.

Another dimension of woman's unique curse has to do with her relationship with man. God informed Eve that under the fallen reality, "Your desire will be for your husband, and he shall rule over you" (Genesis 3:16). In a broken "complement" to man's addictive grasping after work, fallen woman's propensity tends toward relational grasping. Eve was created with a unique relational authority and anointing, but outside of Eden her desire for relationship can easily become a liability instead.

The phrase "your desire will be for your husband" includes an insinuation of competition. Beyond just desiring her husband's attention, this phrase indicates a desire to rule over the man, which makes sense in the light of the passive leadership of Adam and many men who have followed in his footsteps. Created from Adam's side, Eve was made

---

[24] 1 Timothy 2:14
[25] Genesis 3:16

to embody an equal, yet under the curse, she tends to desire power over men or to fear unsafe subjection underneath him.

WOMAN'S CURSE TODAY

The pain of woman's calling, combined with her disordered desires for relationship, have created in our fallen world a host of women who experience dissatisfaction and even despair in unfulfilling relationships. Many women have questioned whether their hearts could ever be satisfied, their desire for intimacy ever fulfilled. The phenomenal success of cheap romance novels speaks to and plays off this insatiable hunger of fallen woman in a world where reality seems to promise only further wounding and disappointment.

As my wife Jordyn entered adolescence, she feared that her unstable emotions were too much. She speaks of often feeling that "It's never okay not to be okay." She struggled to find a relationship where she felt safe to be known, until she found it in an older, married man. As he shared his marriage struggles with Jordyn, she finally felt permission to be emotionally unstable too, and her natural gift for relationship became consumed with a man who could never truly provide what she needed. The relationship denigrated into adultery and became all-consuming, a curse rather than a gift.

For other women, the curse can have myriad manifestations. When she shifts away from faith into a distrust of God, she can become chaotic, hardened, bitter, manipulative, or obsessed with caring for others who are hurting while only feeding off their wounds. Her natural gifts to *be*, *know, and relate* can become liabilities of self-hatred, confusion, and toxic relational idolatry.

MALE AND FEMALE UNDER THE CURSE

In the Garden of Delight (Eden literally means "Delight"), God's desire was the peaceful cohesion and unity of male and female bodies and spirits. Men and women were intended to *feel, act, and believe* in such a way that exhibited complete unity of body and spirit. Created gender was to model both a visible physical characteristic (genitalia as well as a generally unique body) and a spiritual essence corresponding to that gender.

Under the curse, we must delineate between gender and gender identity.[26] How we feel can easily become separated from who we were created to be. What a grief to know that these problems were never part of God's good plan for us. We can deduce from our study of Genesis 3 that gender identity crisis is something common to all humanity, not just those experiencing the more extreme crisis of feeling trapped in a wrongly gendered body.

After the Edenic divide, while created gender is almost always quite clear from birth, gender identity has to do with how one *feels* about being male or female. For a man, gender identity includes how he feels he measures up to manhood – what he believes being a man is all about, and his satisfaction and interest in attaining those believed ideals. My gender insecurity looked like wondering if I would ever measure up to other men and believing that "gay" was the only way I made sense as a man. I have worked with many other men who look to a work promotion to feel they measure up as men, or they will attempt to find a sense of desirability and empowerment from women through the use of heterosexual pornography, often without even acknowledging the humanity of the women they use.

Once in our church, we hosted an event which involved men hearing women share how it felt to live in a world where men leer and sexualize them so often. One woman poignantly shared that she didn't like to jog around her neighborhood because of how often she'd experience a man stop and gawk at her body. After this, one of the men present shared that he had never before understood that his pornography use was hurting people, that it wasn't just enjoying pictures on a screen. He finally understood that in his sin, he cursed the women around him with his lustful posture.

Likewise, women fall into infinite points on a spectrum of what they believe being a woman means for them. Is being a woman safe? Desirable? Does she embody those qualities well or poorly? For Jordyn, gender insecurity looked like finding her value as a woman in a toxic relationship. Others may seek to overcome the dishonor they've received as women by becoming more like men, striving in workaholism to prove an equal value that God has already given them.

---

[26] Joseph Nicolosi, *Shame and Attachment Loss*, p. 18-19

Our church has struggled to know how to best respond to the latest wave of feminism resulting from the election of 2016 and the #MeToo movement. While we celebrate the silence around sexual assault being broken, we've also seen the anger of many women who have felt suppressed or dominated become a source of offense and division. Out of wounding, many seem to separate from the church rather than finding healing in the church. Our best response has been to create spaces where men can hear women verbalize pain and wounds incurred by harmful men, and in prayer, receive honor and healing from the Lord. As men also bring the shame of their abusive behavior to Jesus, we have witnessed remarkable healing as both men and women realize their radical need for Jesus to enable them to walk in honor and unity rather than abuse and offense.

While questions, doubts, fears, and insecurities were never meant to be part of our human experience, we have all struggled with them and have been influenced by lies regarding our given gender and how it speaks to our unique destiny.

HOPE WITHIN THE CURSE

When we begin to perceive just how deep the curse runs in our bodies, our gender, and our sense of worth, it's easy to despair. But even within the curse of Genesis 3 lies a promise. Not only do man and woman receive a curse, but the serpent receives a curse as well — one with eternal impact.

"I will put enmity between you (the serpent) and the woman, and between your offspring and her offspring. He shall bruise your head, and you shall bruise his heel" (Genesis 3:15).

Noteworthy is the great damage humans can inflict upon Satan. Anyone would prefer a heel injury to a head injury. Implicit in this curse are the *ways* in which we can be affected by Satan and the ways in which we can take authority over our enemy. The enemy can only bruise our heels. He can only inflict damage on *how* we walk and live out our humanity; he can never fully decimate the image of God inside of us. However, the offspring of Eve (ultimately Jesus and those He has borne as part of the new creation) have the ability and authority to crush Satan's head, to destroy the very mind of Satan and its influence over our lives. Although insecurity, doubt, and distrust are familiar experiences, they don't have to be the "norm" for the people of God.

When Paul promises a "transformation of the mind,"[27] he is claiming the promised victory of Christ — that no longer must our minds be darkened by the lies and deception of the enemy over our bodies, our gender, and our relationships, but our mindset can exhibit a death-punch to the unholy ministry of Satan and his desired influence over our lives and relationships.

Obviously, this happens over the course of a lifetime. It is the ongoing work of sanctification in light of the reality that a new mind and heart have been paid for by Jesus. This new mind and heart grow in us day by day, as a baby grows inside its mother's womb each day. Every day, we go from "glory to glory"[28] and become a bit more confident in embodying a transformed heart and mind regarding our bodies and genders.

Only one man has ever fully embodied this victorious mindset, this fully unified mind and body within himself and this complete intimacy with God. That man is Jesus. As we seek to re-gain a sense of what our humanity can become, we must begin and end with a study of His life and ministry. We feast on the hope, promises, and example He has given us in His ministry on earth. But, to set the ministry and life of Jesus in context, we first need to understand the laws of God regarding sexuality. This should give us a context in which to understand what Jesus had to say and to whom he said it.

---

[27] Romans 12:1-2
[28] 2 Corinthians 3:18

Chapter Three

WHY THEN THE LAW?

"Why then was the law given? It was added because of transgressions."
Galatians 3:19
"We know that the law is good, if one uses it legitimately."
I Timothy 1:8

After growing up in a conservative Christian home and then experiencing the endorphin-rush of secular college life, I began to see the Law as antiquated, an attempt by "the establishment" to control my life. In truth, I saw God as an authoritarian trying to make me feel guilty, and I wanted out. I talked myself out of these "antiquated rules," which eventually led to me judging Jesus himself as "antiquated" and obsolete.

Today the pull seems a little more subtle. More often than rejecting Christianity, my generation seems to favor keeping Jesus in name but rejecting anything He or His Word says that doesn't align with the secular humanistic values of happiness, permissiveness, and pleasure. "Don't judge" seems to be the only acceptable law. When I hear this ideology, I'm not surprised to find that, before long, Jesus Himself becomes negotiable, inessential, and too "judgy."

Even for those committed to the church, "tolerance" and "acceptance" have become buzzwords that skew the clarity the church is called to offer to a confused world. Some advocate that we celebrate "gay pride" with those who feel that is best for them, while coaching people into Biblical sexual morality if that's what they feel like doing. The new bedrock for justice seems to be what any individual *feels* to be best for them.

On the other side of the coin, however, I've found that as I have surrendered to Jesus, the laws and ways of God have set me free and shown me a best that's far better than what I would ever know to choose for myself. Far from bringing oppression to my life, submitting myself to a higher ethical standard gives me the great gift of *self-control*, the powerful feeling that I **can** choose a way of life that brings me peace, regardless of what my emotional inclination may be. A point of confusion I hear most regularly regarding sexual morality and ethics is this: "We're not under the Law." Sometimes that statement is rephrased to something like "But we don't punish people for eating pork or wearing different kinds of fabric like the law says." The theme or heart-message anytime I hear these statements seems to be, "Why would a loving God put restrictive parameters around who and how we love?" It's a valid question, and we need to explore it a bit in order to understand Jesus's interpretation of the Law.

First, we must put the laws of God into context. Relationship with God preceded the fall of man and continued for hundreds of years before the Law existed. Abraham knew intimacy with God before the law existed; we explicitly know he achieved this friendship with God through faith — through completely entrusting himself to the love and leadership of God.[29] As we'll see, the law came at a unique time in the human experience. Speaking into a world broken by sin, the Law seeks to dignify and protect us from treating one another in dehumanizing ways.

It's important to note that, from a Judaic perspective, the Law — the Torah — isn't just a list of rules. The Torah encompasses the entirety of the first five books of the Bible and contains the history of creation, stories of many men and women as they navigated sin and relationship with God, and climaxes in the Exodus account and the wandering of the children of Israel over 40 years until they reach the Promised Land. In other words, the people of God have historically believed that the Law of God is to believe that Yahweh created us and maintains a loving

---

[29] Romans 4:3

initiative to see His people set free and set into a place of seeing the fulfillment of His good promises over them. Rules and guidelines for life are only a portion of that narrative, albeit the portion that has proven the most troublesome for people of faith over the centuries.

The "rules and guidelines" aspect of the Torah gets set into place at a moment when Israel is going from being an enslaved people to a free people. They had never been in a position to question how to handle their free will because their lives had been controlled by the commands and expectations of their oppressors. They had never had many choices in their lives, but through the deliverance of God, they were about to make a whole plethora of them: choices that affected their handling of land, commerce, politics, clothing, food, and — perhaps most importantly — relationships. All these people had seen was the way life looked for Egyptians, and the life thrust upon them by Egyptians, so they needed another perspective on how to build a loving society. God bestows radical honor upon Israel by giving them another perspective, but not just any perspective: He gives them a vision of the society of Heaven.

In Exodus 26, God gives guidelines for a place of worship and what it should look like — what the representation of heaven on earth would be. He commissioned Bezalel (which literally means "in the shadow of God"), by imparting a vision of heavenly worship, and then commanded him to create on earth exactly what he saw in heaven. Bezalel did that to the best of his ability. It pleased God and resulted in the presence of God manifesting in glory visible to all.[30]

Might we be able to look at God's revelation to Moses regarding His commands for our temples - our bodies - and see a similar desire in our loving God, rather than seeing oppression or attempt at control? Might we believe that the Law's attempt to preserve Life — to keep the picture of love and intimacy intact— is something that came from the same heart as the sacrifice and extravagant love of Jesus?

OUR DISCOMFORT WITH THE LAW

Over the years, I've heard many people talk about the ways of God as expressed in the law as if the God of the Old Testament were some

---

[30] Exodus 40:34

harsh, dictatorial presence, waiting to smite any minor infraction of his senseless rules. Do we really believe that the God who expressed Himself through Jesus would possess another side that is so narrow, so latently angry?

The truth is, the wages of sin have always been death, well before the law came into being. Remember Genesis 3? The very day sin entered the world, physical and spiritual death entered[31] and became a tragic part of humanity. In other words, *sin* killed people, not the law. How could sin not entail death? If the root of sin is a disconnection from trust in God — the source of all life — it only makes sense that a life outside of this trust could only bring death.

In studying the law of God, we find that actually very few issues in it brought about earthly death as punishment. No one was killed or even punished for eating pork. No one was killed or even punished for wearing different types of fabric in their clothing. Like the laws of any nation or household, there were issues that were small and there were a few issues that were large indeed and carried with them a weighty consequence.[32]

Of the "weighty" or non-negotiable issues, none carried greater consequence than two issues: murder and sexual immorality. With regards to murder, all of humanity continues to uphold the gravity of robbing the life of another. On the other hand, with regards to sexual immorality, our culture and even the Church has decided that maybe God was harsh and close-minded about sex, and that maybe we can bless what God cursed nearly as strongly as murder.

What's the connection between murder and sex? How could sex be as big a deal as murder? It's a good question. I've listened to many people fighting for their rights to choose their sexual destiny make comments such as, "It's not like I'm murdering anybody!" These individuals inevitably then compare their sin to eating pork or wearing two different kinds of fabric, as if these issues would be the better comparison-point to their exercise of sexual "freedom." Our enemy has successfully planted the very same doubts and distrust into us that he planted

---

[31] Romans 5:12

[32] For more on Levitical laws regarding sexual ethics, see Robert A. J. Gagnon, *The Bible and Homosexual Practice*, p. 111-146. He specifically finds the word "toebah" that describes homosexuality's "abomination" as something "God hates" (p. 120).

into Adam and Eve: "Did God really say?...You shall not surely die!"

Unfortunately, when it came to sexual immorality, under the law, you would surely die.

The Old Testament law was given to the people of God in a broken system — a world already tarnished by sin. However, through it, Israel could glimpse a life of sonship with God rather than slavery to the world. Likewise, for the redeemed of God today, we can look to His word to show us what the yoke of sonship looks like — how much better it is than the yoke of slavery to lust or worldly ways of "love." Within the law is a promise that we need not be slaves any longer to lust but can live and think differently.

THE HIGH STAKES OF SEX

In murder, the choices of one person deny another person his or her fundamental right to life. Murder merited death because it caused death in another. Likewise, our sexual organs, our genitals, are the parts of our body that can *generate* life.

When we partner this knowledge with the heightened way sexual sin was treated in the law, we can easily deduce that, from God's perspective, our sexuality is also a matter of life and death — it literally defines the way and means by which new life enters the earth. When sexuality is submitted to God and operates within the culture of heaven, new life is brought about in ways that promote love, security, and joy.

When sexuality is submitted only to the subjective experience of an individual's feelings and desires, new life isn't safe. It's blotted out or side-lined rather than elevated in the mind and heart of those of us who were created to bear the image of God — the God who gives Himself to create and nurture new life.

As far as concepts go, this one was the first and most important one I had to grasp as I began to grapple with my sexuality and my confusing, misdirected sexual appetite. A few weeks after surrendering my life to Jesus, I was confused and unclear about how this "yes" to Jesus was supposed to affect my life as a single, gay-identified man. How big of a deal was all this to God?

I am forever grateful that a trustworthy Christian man sat down with me at this early and vulnerable stage of my life as a Christian and, truthfully and candidly shared how Jesus was redeeming his sexuality and calling him up into higher integrity and purity. Then, with such love, belief, and truthful clarity, he looked me in the eye and said, "Andrew, sexuality is a life-and-death issue to God — in His mind it is a big deal what you do with your body."

While many would read this statement and hear only harsh condemnation or the "shaming" we're all so afraid of, in this man's eyes I saw love and belief. His next statement brought the knowledge of the law into the light of the gospel.

"If your sexuality is a life-and-death issue to God, then don't you know that He will move heaven and earth to make sure your restoration is complete and full? If your sexuality is life-and-death to God, that means it's His priority to see you secured into a solid, safe place of integrity and holiness." I knew this meant something different than going from "gay" to "straight" (secular terms we tend to get much too fixated on). He was talking about going from the slavery of lust into a pure, faithful, and integrated way of thinking about people. He was talking about learning to love.

THE WEIGHT OF SIN

If we can truly see our sexual sin as a life-and-death issue, our excuses become a bit more non-sensical. Can you imagine sitting down with someone and saying, "Last week I murdered a few times, but I can tell I'm growing because I didn't feel shame this time." Would it be easy for you to say something like, "I know I have a problem with murder, but life is a little too crazy right now to get counseling — after all, I'm under grace."

To be clear — I am not suggesting that we start a political movement to see adultery or homosexuality be given the death penalty in our local or national laws. I am suggesting that we each fall on our faces before our Holy God and ask Him to give us His eyes for our bodies and His eyes for the weight of our sexual sin. I am suggesting that the sick-stomach feeling after sinning sexually isn't just a result of shame from our conservative religious past. Let us feel that sickness and recognize it for what it is: a grief that we have taken what God has destined for life and prosperity and turned it into an avenue of selfishness and abuse in our pursuit of immediate pleasure. We have taken the part of ourselves (and often the part of someone else, whether virtually or in the flesh) destined to generate life and believed it didn't matter when we used it for our own purposes that were at odds with God's.

WHAT DOES THE BIBLE CALL SEXUAL SIN?

Leviticus 18-20 is a portion of the law that focuses on sexuality. Taken together, these chapters detail what God calls sexual sin and explains these sins' differing severities. So, if our goal is a sexuality that conforms to God's desire for us, a great place to start is this expression of what falls outside of His boundary lines for us.

I take the laws regarding sexuality as a sort of box or parameter. With any sport, the lines within which the game is to be played are essential. Inside the lines of a basketball court, for example, a lot of games could be played that may or may not be basketball. However, basketball is only going to be played inside a basketball court.

Likewise, many people have lived generally within God's boundary lines for sexual expression. That doesn't mean that they are living out the fullness of love — rather, it means is that they're in the ballpark and have the opportunity to enter into the fullness of love. We can know for certain, however, that if we're living outside of God's boundary lines, we aren't even in the game of learning love. The first step is to get inside the court, and then we can begin to learn how to truly love.

So, just what are these boundary lines?[33]

1. **Commitment**. Just as God remains faithful to His Bride, He also asks that our sexuality honor the commitment of marriage. Thus we should not look outside the lines of marital covenant for sexual gratification. This is why adultery is a big deal[34] — it denies the binding of heart that happens in marriage. Fornication[35] is also a big deal because it, likewise, treats sexual activity outside life-long commitment as negotiable. I've known so many people devastated by the "yes" they gave to someone, assuming it was going to be a lasting relationship only to have their sexual partner move on to someone else, thereby dishonoring the unique bonding meant to happen in a sexual experience between a man and woman for life.

---

[33] The outline of commitment, complementarity, and boundary taken from Andrew Comiskey, *Living Waters: Pursuing Sexual and Relational Wholeness in Christ* (2007 edition).

[34] Exodus 20:14

[35] Exodus 22:16-17

2. **Complementarity**.[36] From the creation of Adam and Eve onward, we see God's heart for man to have a partner "corresponding to him."[37] The Mosaic Law expounds on what corresponds and what doesn't and which appropriate dynamic of similarity and dissimilarity creates true companionship for man and woman. In Leviticus 18:23, beastiality is outlawed — it's exposed to be outside of the realm of discovering God's way of love. Why? Animals have dissimilarity to men and women, and no corresponding similarity that reproduces life after humanity's unique dimensions.

In addition, incest is outlawed[38] — it is exposed to be outside of the realm of discovering God's way of love. Why? Family members have similarity — often both physically and emotionally. Immediate family members exhibit remarkable likeness because they come from the same gene pool. From God's perspective, however, family members don't have a corresponding dissimilarity that reproduces a life of loving that which is different and "other than" oneself.

On these same terms, homosexuality is likewise outlawed[39] — it is exposed to be outside the realm of discovering God's way of love. Homosexual couples have similarity — both physically and emotionally; two men have the same essential make-up as one another. From God's perspective, however, members of the same gender don't have a corresponding dissimilarity that reproduces life by awakening a love for that which is different and "other than" oneself. Homosexuality too falls outside of the court of love.

3. **Boundary**.Boundary involves respecting the unique beginning and end of oneself as a sexual, gendered creature, while also respecting the unique boundary lines of someone else's humanity. It's respecting where I end and someone else's unique life and dignity begin. Boundary enters the equation when the Law talks about rape.[40] Rape denies another person the dignity of choice. It's treating someone else's body as if it were mine to utilize as I wish.

---

[36] For in-depth material on gender complementarity in the creation accounts, see Gagnon, *The Bible and Homosexual Practice*, page 61.

[37] Genesis 2:18

[38] Leviticus 18:6

[39] Leviticus 18:22

[40] Deut. 22:26

Boundary also enters the equation regarding transgenderism and its underlying heart-issue of gender dysphoria that we see so often today.[41] The choice to identify and engage as the opposite gender denies the reality of the boundary lines God has crafted within each of our bodies. To say, "My body only expresses maleness, but I'd prefer it to express femaleness," is a denial of the gift of the unique, defined body and spirit God gave each of us. Like rape denies another human's choice, transgenderism denies God the choice of which gender He intended for me and puts that choice into my own hands. It's treating my body as if it were mine to utilize as I wish, rather than God's. In thinking through other forms of sexual expression, we do well to use this same grid: Am I treating my body as though it were mine to do with as I wish, or am I using the mind of Christ and seeking the way He looks out for others' very best?

THE TEN COMMANDMENTS

Across all of Orthodox Judeo-Christianity for thousands of years, the Ten Commandments have been elevated as the clearest distillation of the law of God and the most succinct expression of His heart in the Old Testament.

A few years ago, I learned something fascinating about how Jews teach the Ten Commandments that helped clarify the way God sees our relationship with Him and others as connected. In some circles of Orthodox Judaism, the Ten Commandments are lined up in two columns of five commandments each. On one side, you see five commandments that describe sins against our trust in God. (If you do this exercise, you'll see that from a Jewish perspective, honoring our parents isn't a question of our trust and love for our parents, but an issue of our trust in the authority and trustworthiness of God.) When you line up the second group of five commandments, you'll see the way we treat one another as paralleling how we treat God.

Again, at the top of the list of human breakdowns stands murder. It aligns with the first commandment: That we will have no other gods before Jehovah. In other words, just as we cannot forget and blot out the life of God, neither can we take it upon ourselves to blot out the life of another human being.

---

[41] Deuteronomy 22:5

What do you guess is the issue next in line as far as relational importance? You got it — adultery. "Thou shalt not commit adultery" is a statement that most Bible scholars believe doesn't just entail sexual relations with someone other than a spouse, but is an encapsulation of the entire Mosaic Law regarding sexual morality. In other words, "Thou shalt not commit adultery" reads easier and clearer than saying "Thou shalt pay attention to the pages and chapters of my law that have to do with proper sexual relations."

If sexual integrity is second only to murder in priority, what is the corresponding heart-issue with God? It is found in the second commandment — the prohibition of idolatry. The most hurtful thing we could do to God is to blot out His name, forget Him, and deny Him in our hearts, which would be like attempting to murder Him. The second most hurtful thing we can do to God is to worship Him while simultaneously worshipping idols or created things, which would be like adultery. The sin of idolatry says, "God — you're worthy of worship and I love you. I want you. But I also love these other things and want them too. What I just don't want to do is choose. Can't I have both You and the things of this world at the same time? It's not like I'm denying You exist!" God makes clear that these "other things" can be any created thing. And the creature that God has made most beautiful, and thus most prone to being idolized, is the human being.

So when we have an idolatrous heart-posture, our relationship with God is affected and thus our human relationships are doomed to be likewise affected. An adulterous heart says the same thing to a human that an idolatrous heart says to God. The adulterous heart says, "I know my body was made for covenant, and I do love you (a current or future spouse). However, at this moment of time, I want someone or something else (a sexual fantasy or partner), too. What I just don't want is to choose. I don't really have to choose, do I? Can't I have both purity and lustful pleasure at the same time? It's not like I'm committing murder!"

When we see things laid out, bare and open before the eyes of God, it can be scary. The reality of our shameful rationalizations and our unfaithfulness to our Creator can feel overwhelming. And it is overwhelming — let us not try to minimze it. Either we will allow this revelation to cast us onto the Rock of Jesus and cry out for mercy or we will ourselves harden even more until we must be broken to pieces again.[42] The moment I felt the weight of my sexual immorality and allowed myself to face my unfaithfulness and lust-filled heart was the moment my transformation began.

The writer of Hebrews gives us important revelation of how to respond once we find that the Word of God has exposed our darkness:

> *For the word of God is living and active, sharper than any two-edged sword, piercing to the division of soul and of spirit, of joints and of marrow, and discerning the thoughts and intentions of the heart. And no creature is hidden from his sight, but all are naked and exposed to the eyes of him to whom we must give account.*
>
> *Since then we have a great high priest who has passed through the heavens, Jesus, the Son of God, let us hold fast our confession. For we do not have a high priest who is unable to sympathize with our weaknesses, but one who in every respect has been tempted as we are, yet without sin. Let us then with confidence draw near to the throne of grace, that we may receive mercy and find grace to help in time of need. (Hebrews 4:11-16)*

Rather than engage in theological gymnastics to try to prove that we need not feel exposed by scripture, we have this merciful exhortation to bring our shame and exposure to Jesus and find *help and hope* to become different. To experience the way this transformation occurs, we need to look to the life of the One who is our high priest — Jesus.

---

[42] Matthew 21:44

Chapter Four

JESUS, THE REDEEMER OF OUR BODIES

*Through the fact that the Word of God became flesh, the body entered
theology . . . through the main door."*
Pope John Paul II

We offer a support group in my church called Living Waters for
anyone seeking a better way to live in intimacy. It's been a phenomenal
success — every time one of our 20-week programs ends, we hear story
after story of individuals in our church learning to live in the powerful
duality of faith and vulnerability, to hold onto the truth and mercy of
Jesus as they learn to become truthful and merciful themselves.

Beyond any other reason that Living Waters works is the fact that
every week centers on the crucifixion and resurrection of Jesus. As we
learn to live in the rhythm of the cross and the empty tomb, we become
transformed into the image of Jesus and learn to love like He loves us.

For a Christian, the crucifixion and resurrection of Jesus is central
to every aspect of life. The fact that sins, wounds, and false beliefs have
died with Christ, and a new spiritually-unified life has been imparted to
us, changes and defines everything. Paul put words around a new way
of being human: "I have been crucified with Christ, and it is no longer I
who live. Jesus Christ now lives in me" (Galatians 2:20).

Most particularly, as we find the meaning of our bodies and the inte-
gration of our physical and spiritual desires, we cannot move beyond
this revelation that Christ has gone before us, dying to sin and rising
bodily through the power of the Holy Spirit. We now seek to receive

greater revelation of the life, death, and resurrection of Jesus through the lens of the created intention for our bodies and the legal expectations around our humanity.

Let's recap where we've been. We've seen the beauty and glory of God's creation and its pinnacle in the creation of the human body — particularly in its' capacity to achieve an intimacy after God's own self-giving spirit, soul and body.

We uncovered the glory of male and female in all their inherent differences — the way that, in intimacy together, we can begin to see the love and nature of God who is lion and lamb, father and mother, justice and mercy.

Then we unpacked the multiple dimensions of the curse that came upon Adam, Eve, and all the rest of us. We saw how, rather than an intimate harmony that reveals God, our sexuality and gender have become perverted, dirtied by judgment, lust, and abuse of one another. We saw how the curse affects men and women differently, yet in equally powerful brokenness.

In light of our proclivity to pervert and use others, thus distorting the image of God, we saw how God instated His laws and ways to give us a framework to understand "the ballpark" or boundary lines of where our sexuality can and cannot reveal His love to others. We saw that, although adherence to the boundaries God instated is essential to finding His pure way of loving, adherence to the law by no means equals achieving intimacy or embodying God's self-giving spirit, soul, and body.

So, we find ourselves in the same spot people with a knowledge of the law have found themselves in since time began. It's great to understand our potential and insightful to understand our boundaries, but it is equally convicting and depressing to understand just how far we've fallen, just how tainted our desire for love can be.

In short, we need a Savior. In His life on earth, Jesus embodied both *true justice* in His elevated vision of healthy love, and *true mercy* in his transformative relationships with broken people.

OUR HERO ARRIVES ON THE SCENE

Through Jesus, God fully enters our broken world. Born in a barn, from day one–the presence of Jesus assures us that He'll choose to be with us wherever we'll give Him a place — in the midst of our mess, transforming a dirty animal trough into something glorious, simply because He's there.

The first public sermon Jesus gave hit on the distortion of sexuality in a clear and convicting way:

"You have heard that it was said, 'You shall not commit adultery'. But I say to you that everyone who looks at a woman with lustful intent has already committed adultery with her in his heart" (Matthew 5:27-28).

Right off the bat, we know that Jesus isn't satisfied with outward conformity to the law of Moses. In essence, He says, "not having illicit sex isn't the answer — your heart needs a redirection, a transformation away from seeing people as objects of usefulness."

True? Yes. Easy? No. In this discourse Jesus doesn't give much practical advice for how to walk in a different mindset; He strictly reveals the conundrum man is already in with regard to lust. So, while this brief introduction to the mind of Jesus shows His understanding of the depths of lust we all have experienced, we're left wondering how He practically would treat us if He saw our junky hearts.

THE WELL AT SAMARIA

With that in mind, let's look at John 4 and Jesus's transforming conversation with the Samaritan woman.

In this scene, we have a woman with whom we can identify. She's been in multiple broken relationships, yet Jesus initiates conversation with her. Quickly, he exposes her relational dysfunction, and just as quickly, she tries to change the subject to religious pietism. She'd rather talk about the proper scenery for worship rather than her quiet despair for intimacy. Again, cutting through to clarity, Jesus reveals to this woman His biggest secret — His identity as Messiah. Because we know the end of the story, we can forget the scandal: to this broken woman comes one of the very first full disclosures Jesus has given of His Messianic role. In other words, Jesus exposes this woman's misdirected desire for intimacy and exchanges it for an intimate disclosure of Himself. The result? Lit on fire with a new kind of passion, she tells everyone in her town about His knowledge and power to such an extent that the whole town comes to believe in the man who revealed Himself to this woman they knew. This Samaritan woman became the first power-evangelist.

JESUS AND THE ADULTERER

Another scene occurs in John 8, in the very temple of God.

"The scribes and the Pharisees brought a woman who had been caught in adultery and placing her in their midst they said to him, 'Teacher, this woman has been caught in the act of adultery. Now in the Law, Moses commanded us to stone such women. So what do you say?'" (John 8:3-5).

Again, Jesus has a known sexual misfit right in front of Him. In this scene, Jesus takes His time to give a proper response to the mess in front of Him. He seems to hesitate, scribbling on the ground. He asks for the person who has a truly clean heart to begin the condemnation of the woman so clearly unclean. After they all leave, only Jesus is left. He is the one man able to make a judgment regarding this woman, as He is the one man truly innocent of lust of the heart. Instead of condemnation, Jesus responds to this woman with compassion. "Neither will I condemn you" (John 8:11). His next statement, "Go and sin no more" (v. 11), goes beyond compassion to a plea for transformation. Knowing this man chose to save her life, the woman is invited into a new kind of life.

Remember how God created the world? Through His spoken word. What He spoke became reality. I believe that when Jesus spoke "Go and sin no more," along with that invitation and plea, there was also an *impartation*: a new lifestyle and way of living and loving made available to this woman simply through the spoken word of Jesus.

JESUS POINTS TO THE BEGINNING

We find an essential key in discerning Jesus' view of human sexuality and relationships in His comments on marriage.[43] When confronted with the permission Moses gave husbands to send their wives away with an official statement of divorce if she displeased him or he was ready to move on, Jesus answers in a statement packed with meaning:

"It was because of your hardness of heart that Moses permitted you to be divorced, but **it was not this way from the beginning**" *(Matthew 19:8, emphasis added).*[44]

---

[43] Matthew 19:9, Mark 10:11, and Luke 16:18

[44] For Jesus's appeal to the beginning as a focus for sexual ethics, see Gagnon, *The Bible and Homosexual Practice*, p. 193ff, and John Paul II, *TOB*, 10:3. Much of TOB hinges on Christ's appeal to "the beginning".

Rather than hash through details of the Mosaic law, Jesus appeals to the beginning — Eden — God's original plan for human relationships before sin and distrust entered the picture. Later in the New Testament, Paul will go to great lengths to describe the superseding power of God's will over the specifics of the Law, but here, with a simple phrase, Jesus communicates this concept masterfully. Rather than looking to what we are or aren't allowed to do by the Law, Jesus appeals to our hearts to look to the will of God from the beginning — to see what we're made for and to direct our lives accordingly.

If we carry this thought through, so many issues that have become confusing get simplified. Divorce becomes clear when viewed through this lens, as Adam and Eve become inseparably (not temporarily) one. Homosexuality becomes clear, as the two in the beginning were made in God's image, male and female. The brokenness of isolation becomes clear in comparison to the beginning, as God expressed, "It is not good for man to be alone," (Genesis 2:18).

When we pair Jesus's teachings on righteousness with the heart of power and mercy expressed to the woman at the well and the woman caught in adultery, we begin to get a picture of a man who is absolutely challenging in his exacting view of what our bodies were made for, yet utterly extravagant in showing mercy to those who are crushed by their struggles and failures in relationships. His goal seems to be to get us to realize our disastrous choices made out of our needs and felt desires and to draw us to a place of surrendering our ideas to Him and throwing ourselves onto a power stronger than our lustful desire for fulfillment so that we can learn a new way of living and loving.

For church leaders today to experience the fruit of leading people in the way of Jesus, we too must embrace the duality of a high challenge to repent from our fleshly tendency to use and abuse others for our own gain and pair that challenge with extravagant mercy for those walking through the long and messy process of redemption. We must be willing to welcome the struggler into repentance over and over again, while never apologizing for the call to reject sinful ways of relating. *This* is how we model the ministry of Jesus to a generation who needs mercy, clarity, and strength to enter into true love.

CELIBACY

In Matthew 19 Jesus introduces another concept into the conversation of sexuality and marriage. Jesus's disciples reply perceptively to His call to life-long marital commitment by expressing that true, lifelong, heart-level monogamy sounds more difficult than remaining single.

Jesus replied, "Not everyone can accept this word, but only those to whom it has been given. For there are eunuchs who were born that way, and there are eunuchs who have been made eunuchs by others — and there are those who choose to live like eunuchs for the sake of the kingdom of heaven. The one who can accept this should accept it" (Matthew 19:11-12).

I love that Jesus doesn't try to argue that marriage can be easy or that singleness can be easy. Rather, he expresses that, yes — joining to a person of the opposite gender for a life of chosen commitment and devotion is difficult, in some ways more difficult than remaining single. He also expresses a potential for some to choose celibacy as a lifestyle in order to be devoted to the kingdom of heaven. Only some can accept this way of life joyfully, but those who can are participating in something quite valuable.

In this passage, Jesus is talking about three different scenarios, each with different causes, results, and value statements. In describing a eunuch who was "born that way," Jesus describes people who bear birth defects causing sterility. Some such birth defects we know of today would be intersex genetic mutations, Kleinfelters syndrome, or other genital mutations. He does not express that people with difficulty relating to others or who experience conflictual sexual desires should accept these difficulties as their lot in life.

Jesus expresses the reality that some people are born with physical deformities that preclude them from being able to procreate. He doesn't say this is good or bad. The statement recalls what Jesus says in John 9 about the man born blind. It wasn't that the man was born blind because he was bad, or his parents were bad; it was so the power of God could be revealed through a creative miracle. Similar to how God's intention would be for the healing of someone born without functional eyes, it's an easy step to believe that God's intention is for the healing of someone born without functional genitals.

The second scenario Jesus describes are those made eunuchs by others. These are individuals who, oppressed by empirical brutality, had their genitals cut off without their choice. Biblically, we know that Daniel, Shadrach, Meshach, and Abednego were such men who were forced into servitude in a way that likely included their emasculation.[45]

To such individuals who have endured this torture, the prophet Isaiah gives a beautiful promise:

> Let not the foreigner who has joined himself to the Lord say,
>   "The Lord will surely separate me from his people";
> and let not the eunuch say,
>   "Behold, I am a dry tree."
> For thus says the Lord:
> "To the eunuchs who keep my Sabbaths,
>   who choose the things that please me
>   and hold fast my covenant,
> I will give in my house and within my walls
>   a monument and a name
>   better than sons and daughters;
> I will give them an everlasting name
>   that shall not be cut off.
> Isaiah 56:3-5

Again, Jesus doesn't make an evaluative statement about forced "eunuch-hood," but from His treatment of others who are oppressed, we can assume His advocacy and desire to bring a dignified, fulfilling life and legacy to those who have endured mistreatment or torture of any kind.

The third kind of "eunuch-hood" is separate from a birth defect or torturous abuse. These are individuals who choose to forego the picture that marriage is of God's desire to unite with humanity, and who choose to enter into a special union with God that precludes marriage for the sake of an undivided attention to advancing the kingdom and purposes of God. Paul echoes this — those who marry do well, and those who forego marriage to enter into union with God for the sake of building up the church do even better.[46]

---

[45] Daniel 1:3, 7
[46] 1 Corinthians 7:38

We must recognize that Jesus doesn't evaluate whether singlehood or marriage is better or worse, but simply states that some can accept life-long singleness for the purpose of devotion to God, and others cannot, and only those who can accept this celibacy and choose it joyfully should pursue it.

JESUS'S RELATIONSHIPS

Beyond Jesus's words and extraordinary encounters with those in need of forgiveness and sexual restoration, we have record of the way Jesus related as a man choosing earthly celibacy. His was not a life without intimacy or a life lived waiting for the right person to date or marry. Jesus gave His years on earth to spiritually "father" others and raise them up to carry on His legacy in the same way many men intentionally raise their biological children. In the intimacy of the Last Supper, we see a man who purely and passionately loved His friends, imparting fatherly vision and wisdom and giving physical care and affection through the washing of their feet in a way that was power-fully intimate yet devoid of sexual overtones. His ultimate exhortation to these spiritual children is found in John 13-17, a magnum opus on the expression of love.

Jesus begins not with words but with action: He washes the disci-ple's dirtiest parts — their feet. He physically expresses love to them and serves them in a way only attributed to slaves. With His actions, Jesus is saying that true love is unafraid to serve in ways that seem demeaning. Then, with His words, Jesus gives his friends one lasting commandment — that they love one another in the same powerful, extravagant way.[47] A friend can lay his head against Jesus's chest and hear secrets from his heart openly in the presence of a crowd.[48]

Jesus is unafraid and unashamed to love intimately and purely. In fact, in this last meal, Jesus offers communion to his disciples in terms that are intended to recall marriage vows: "This is my body, which is given for you."[49] To answer our hunger for love, Jesus gives us His body as a source of never-ending spiritual intimacy.

---

[47] John 13:14
[48] John 13:25
[49] Luke 22:19

THE KING IS DEAD

Jesus reveals His visionary love, but that love is rejected by Israel. Instead, Jesus must endure all the things that Adam and Eve ushered in: judgment, undeserved criticism, mockery, sarcasm, abuse. He is stripped naked and is publicly exposed, no doubt eliciting impure glances mixed with haughty mockery. And He endures. At no point does Jesus decide the pain just isn't worth it. He "loved them to the very end,"[50] no matter the cost. And He suffered the ultimate cost of relationship with a fallen humanity: the pain of having His own people choose to distrust Him, and desire to both control and supersede Him.

The cross is essential to the life of every Christian. To worship Jesus wholeheartedly, we must understand the power of this substitutionary death. My sins of sexual assault, pornography, and degradation of my God-given gender have all died and been punished through this death. Every wound of abuse, abandonment, rejection, and dishonor has been taken by Jesus and rendered powerless through Him. Every other self-definition (addict, victim, trans-, gay, polyamorous) has died and a new claim has been made for my life: I belong to Jesus, am radically loved by Him, and am identified with His definition of me.

THE KING LIVES

Ultimately, the supreme hope and belief of Christianity has always been in what happened next. Resurrecting from the dead, Jesus inhabits His body in a way unseen before. Very much alive and at home in a body, Jesus's resurrected flesh has abilities and capacities that hadn't yet been experienced. He could walk through walls. He could seem invisible to those who knew him before yet be unmistakably recognizable when those same people looked at Him in a different way. Both to His friends on the road to Emmaus and to His disciples while fishing, Jesus was never more clearly revealed as Himself as He was in the sharing of food — an undeniably *bodily* act.[51]

As the crucifixion claims us, so the resurrection defines our lives as Christians. I no longer need to identify with old sins, wounds, and self-definitions because the life of Jesus Himself is now being lived

---

[50] John 13:1; Hebrews 12:2
[51] Luke 24:30-31; John 21:9-14

through my body. Just as Jesus's body revealed His resurrected glory, so too can my body show the love of Christ as I serve Him rather than seek my own service or pleasure through my mouth, hands, and body. Like Paul, we can proclaim, "I have been crucified with Christ, and it is no longer I who live. Jesus Christ now lives in me" (Galatians 2:20).

This part is important. For too long, Christianity has treated the desires of the body as something less than spiritual, as something suspicious. But Jesus is most fully and clearly Himself when He's eating earthly food and sharing human fellowship. He gets his mouth up close to his friends and breathes on them to receive the Holy Spirit[52] — an undeniably physical encounter and simultaneously a potent spiritual experience.

Remember how man was created? God formed his body, then *breathed* into his nostrils to create man's spirit. Spiritual unity with God was compromised in Eden. But now, with resurrection authority, Jesus breathes back into the nostrils of His followers the Holy Spirit of eternal life.

After a season of encountering multiple people on earth in His resurrected body, Jesus leaves his disciples with a commission: to represent and reproduce this new way of living, this Kingdom lifestyle, into all the earth.[53]

Finally, we have a vision for what humanity can be, the spiritual renewal to make this our own way of life, and the capacity to reproduce this Kingdom life until it fills the earth. This is our amazing hope! Through His life, crucifixion, and resurrection, Jesus revealed a whole new horizon for what it means to be human.

I was recently talking to a friend who spoke beautifully of this revelatory ministry of Jesus. After a childhood filled with sexual abuse by her churchgoing father, Susie sought much counseling and other resources as a way to survive after such trauma. After a season of healing in our church centered around the crucifixion and resurrection, Susie was able to smile and express how the cross had become a *home* for her — a place to bring her pain and trauma and see it absorbed in the pain and trauma that God Himself endured. She began to see a

---

[52] John 20:22
[53] Matthew 28:18

resurrected, new kind of life available to her, every day a bit freer from the clouds of disappointment, bitterness, and cynicism. Her new life is marked by hope, joy, and expectation of greater things to come. *This* is what Jesus died for — that the defilement and pain of our past might no longer define us, but that a new horizon and way of living would open up before our eyes as we step ever closer to paradise.

Chapter Five

WHAT HAPPENED
NEXT

"Those who indulge in sexual sin, or who worship idols, or commit
adultery, or are male prostitutes, or practice homosexuality, or are
thieves, or greedy people, or drunkards, or are abusive, or cheat peo-
ple—none of these will inherit the Kingdom of God. Some of you were
once like that. But you were cleansed; you were made holy; you were
made right with God by calling on the name of the Lord Jesus Christ
and by the Spirit of our God."
I Corinthians 6:9-11 (NLT)

Applying the truths of God's word and the ultimate truth of Jesus's crucifixion and resurrection to everyday life has been the heartbeat of my work in the church since I entered vocational ministry. For any pastor, this is his purpose and our joy.

However, in the decade since I became a Christian and began pastoring others, the cultural landslide of moral relativism has threatened to compromise our commitment to this calling. On the surface, it may seem that a politically correct and inoffensive posture toward sexuality and gender is necessary to have influence in our world today. However, this passivity and tolerance, so much the new expectation for church leaders, leads not only to a compromise of our moral fiber but also to a lessening of our power to proclaim the death and resurrection of Jesus as the central answer to every type of brokenness. Once the central answer becomes passivity and tolerance rather than crucifixion and resurrection, we've become a flaccid organization, certainly not the kind of church that defeats the gates of hell.

The cost is becoming dearer to those who choose integrity, and the seductive pull of public approval is becoming more enticing than ever. My church has seen and felt grievous fallout as we've made clear our stance for Jesus to define our bodies and relationships. Church members who once sang our praises as a place to find freedom from empty religion have left and now accuse us of being intolerant and bigoted.

The stakes are as high as they've ever been. Do we want to be part of a social club in which anyone feels content, or do we want to give our lives for the establishment of a Kingdom of truth, justice, and powerful mercy, no matter the public perception?

The main reason I remain deeply committed to proclaiming the gospel as it applies to sexual sin, is that this is the kind of clear spiritual environment that made a way for me to be set free. I wasn't helped by people telling me to do whatever I felt was best. I was helped by a community and church who had the guts to look at me and say, "Jesus has better for you, and we will believe that for you when you are too weak to believe it for yourself." In my early days of learning to love, I was gifted with a community who embodied both crucifixion-gravity (our sin kills Jesus) and resurrection-joy (His Spirit sets us free). I'm filled with concern today when I think of how few churches have this gravity, joy, and support to offer those struggling with any type of sin. So even though it's costly and unpopular, it is my absolute joy to fight for our church to embody truthful mercy and promote holy love, to see the church shine with resurrection joy.

I believe that when we look at the life, relationships, and teachings of Jesus we can see clearly His intention to uphold and strengthen sexual ethics, while simultaneously doing something that had never been done before in creating a way to renew a lifestyle of partnership with God in our bodily humanity. At the onset of the 21st century, however, a theological shift has occurred in which many Christian leaders promote a message in the name of Jesus that is quite different. In light of this, we do well to examine how the fathers of the church interpreted His vision of sexuality and redemption. The apostles built the church with a burning conviction of the importance of our sexual choices and the ability of Holy Spirit to transform all who believe.

THE FIRE OF PENTECOST

Most of us are probably familiar with the big events following Jesus's ascent into heaven. At the feast of Pentecost, the apostles are filled with the fire of the Spirit of God, and a sort of reversal happens among the people gathered in Jerusalem. You see, Pentecost was historically the Jewish celebration of the giving of the Law of Moses. Tongues of fire surrounded Mt. Sinai, and God's heart of justice was made known but was revealed to those whose hearts were unwilling and unable to receive the invitation He was offering. At Sinai, the request of the people receiving the revelation of God's heart was to ask Moses to make it stop. "You go talk to God," they said in essence, "we'd rather keep our distance." When Moses returned with a translation for the people, their immediate descent into idolatry — their inability to say "'yes'" to worshiping Him alone — led to the death of 3,000.[54] It was a sign of the result of the Law — a powerful revelation, no doubt, but not helpful in actually imparting the ability to relate to God intimately.

Since the instatement of the Law of God, people had gathered in Jerusalem each year from all over the world to remember this momentous occasion. But on the holiday immediately following the resurrection of Jesus, tongues of fire descended, not onto Mount Zion, but onto *people*. As the fire descended, the people of God heard a new revelation: not only the justice of God, but also the mercy of God, expressed to each in his own language. As the message of mercy and the powerful implications of the crucifixion and resurrection of Jesus fell onto the people, the result was an exact inverse of the original Pentecost: rather than 3,000 slaughtered by the reality of sin, 3,000 are saved from their sin and are baptized into a new kind of living (Acts 2:41). What had begun as the unique lifestyle of Jesus, in a day, became a movement that would forever change the course of history.

What we know of the early church is that their primary dilemma had to do with the diversity of people coming to faith. On one hand, many Orthodox Jews were coming to believe that Jesus was the promised Messiah, finding the fulfillment and lifeblood of the faith they'd

---

[54] Exodus 32:28

carried for generations. From this fold were all the apostles as well as Paul, who most assuredly found in Jesus not a change in moral expectations but an impartation of God's justice into the heart of man in a way that caused a *living* knowledge of the laws of God versus a merely intellectual one.

Others, too, were coming to faith in Jesus – people without a knowledge of Judaism, people whose experiences had nothing to do with Sinai but rather the pagan idolatry and secular culture of the Greco-Roman world. Their conversions came as a great surprise to the many early Christians whose background was in traditional Judaism. The early church was asking itself how to lead new believers from such exotic backgrounds. What expectations were reasonable to put on people who had no knowledge of the law of Moses? Clearly, the laws and traditions that had been imparted to Jews from birth couldn't be understood by those coming from a pagan background in a matter of days or even years. How much did someone need to know, to understand, to obey, before they could be fully welcomed into the family?

PETER'S VISION

In the midst of these questions, the recognized leader of the Christian sect of Judaism, Peter, had an experience that changed everything. Confronted with a secular man named Cornelius who was interested in following Jesus, Peter prepared himself to reject an invitation to dinner out of fear of becoming aligned with paganism.

The Holy Spirit came upon Peter in a dream that seems on the surface to deal with food. Peter felt like Jesus was asking him to eat food that was forbidden for Jews. As Peter protested, Jesus communicated that if He calls something clean, then it should not be called dirty. Peter's takeaway was that once a person has said "yes" to the love of Jesus, they are no longer unclean in His eyes and are to be accepted into the family of God.[55]

THE COUNCIL OF JERUSALEM

Soon after this vision, the leaders of the Christian sect of Judaism converged in Jerusalem,[56] where Paul was also present — one whose

---

[55] Acts 10:28
[56] Acts 15:1-35

background was steeped in Orthodoxy but was seeing waves of secular Greeks express faith in Jesus. The central question of the council was what a reasonable expectation should be for people without knowledge of morality. Obviously, for someone without background in the intricate moral fabric of Judaism, full understanding of holiness wouldn't come immediately. So, what were the "deal-breakers" and what issues could be sidelined until new believers came into greater understanding of mature morality?

Their decisions? Rejecting idolatry was a no-brainer. For someone to follow Jesus would mean rejecting other objects as worthy of worship. Second to a rejection of idolatry, refraining from sexual immorality was deemed non-negotiable. Remember, from a Jewish perspective, idolatry and sexual immorality are inexorably linked. The Greek word for "sexual immorality" used here and elsewhere in the New Testament is *porneo*, the same word that we use for pornography today. This is a far-reaching term that covers a host of immoral sexual behaviors. The apostles don't detail what exactly they mean by "sexual immorality." For a leader in a first-century Jewish community, *"porneo"* encompassed the entirety of the Mosaic law regarding sexual immorality.[57]

The apostles also asked new believers from pagan backgrounds to abstain from meat that had been unethically killed through strangulation and from eating blood directly. As it pertains to our study of sexuality from a New Testament perspective, the apostles' stance goes something like, "Many aspects of Christianity can be figured out over time, but quickly learn proper sexual ethics and turn away from any version of sexual immorality — it's of utmost importance."

A quick question here — doesn't this decision seem quite different from how church leaders handle people confused in their sexuality today? If there's one bothersome theme I hear consistently regarding pastoral application of sexual morality, it's that we must patiently and passively allow believers to figure out what God wants for their bodies on their own. We are often afraid of being too hasty in expecting people to forsake sexual immorality, but the church fathers in the book of Acts don't buy into this fear. In their eyes, a clear call to repentance is loving a new believer well by rescuing them from death.

---

[57] Gagnon, *The Bible and Homosexual Practice*, p. 116

PAUL'S PASTORAL PROBLEMS

What exactly were new Christians being asked to walk away from sexually? The clearest picture comes from Paul's first letter to the Corinthian church. The Corinthians lived in a culture not unlike America today: cosmopolitan, highly educated, generally wealthy, and steeped in an anything-goes sexual ethic. Corinthians were used to doing what felt good and exerting intellectual and philosophical gymnastics to justify that behavior.

In the midst of this culture, Paul called people to a new way of life. In 1 Corinthians 6, he urges the Corinthians not to be deceived. He wants them to understand that the absence of holiness regarding sexual ethics is not okay — it is not just a flaw to be overlooked with patience.

> Or do you not know that the unrighteous will not inherit the kingdom of God? Do not be deceived: neither the sexually immoral, nor idolaters, nor adulterers, nor men who practice homosexuality, nor thieves, nor the greedy, nor drunkards, nor revilers, nor swindlers will inherit the kingdom of God. And such were some of you. But you were washed, you were sanctified, you were justified in the name of the Lord Jesus Christ and by the Spirit of our God.
> 1 Corinthians 6:9-11

Of note here is that, in Greek, Paul uses two words that are together translated into English as "men who practice homosexuality". The two Greek words describe both the "active/giving" and "passive/receiving" partner involved in homosexual activity.[58] It's only logical, then, to assume that Paul couldn't be *only* describing acts of homosexual rape, unless we believe that Paul is saying that being a victim of rape morally excludes someone from the people of God.

There are two aspects of this passage that stick out to me. One is that, far from a "tolerant" inclusiveness of people in sexual confusion, Paul brings a blessed clarity that God has a definite plan for sexuality. The multiple avenues of sexual expression that secular or religious culture can justify are not the way of the Kingdom of God.

The second aspect of this passage highlights great hope to me. From

---

[58] Gagnon, *The Bible and Homosexual Practice*, pages 303-332

the very earliest days of the church, Paul had the passionate conviction that the church's sacraments — cleansing water, the sanctifying journey of holiness, and the justification miraculously imparted through the Holy Spirit — could bring a complete, transforming change to people of variously broken backgrounds. His clear "you were… but now" signifies concrete change on earth and in heaven.

Many other New Testament passages echo this juxtaposition of black-and-white prophetic unction and radically hopeful expectancy for transformation. Jude describes those who "give themselves to sexual immorality" as deserving "eternal fire" but ends his brief letter with the hope that Jesus can cause us to stand in the glory of His presence, blameless and with extravagant joy.[59]

The writer of Hebrews 12:16-22 uses similar language. The author compares people who disobey biblical commands regarding sexual morality to Esau, whose inability to control his appetites and desires led to him losing an eternal inheritance. The writer then describes the surpassing access we have to the Holy Spirit. He says, "You haven't come to a mountain with fire around it, unable to be touched. You've come to Mount Zion, to a joyful assembly." Freedom can be accessed. Joy can be known and lived in our day.

There are many other examples of this juxtaposition in the New Testament writings of Paul, John, and Peter.[60] The theme is that, on one hand, there's a heightened awareness of the consequences of getting the "picture" of sexuality wrong. No longer are the consequences just temporary. Because we have access to a greater revelation of eternity, the consequences of disobedience are eternal.

The emphasis Paul and the other New Testament writers place on sexuality is what motivates me to place a high emphasis on promoting clear and regular opportunities for members of our church to learn about sexuality, confess their sins, ask their questions, and get support as they pursue healthy and holy relationships. The fruit has been amazing. Church members have shared about secret sins being exposed and then losing their power. Hopelessness is replaced by great faith and vulnerability. At the close of our latest support group, one woman shared, "We always say the church is family, but this environment of talking about

---

[59] Jude 4, 7, 24
[60] e.g. Acts 17:30, 1 Corinthians 5:1-2, Romans 1:18ff, 1 Timothy 1:9-10, Galatians 5

the most intimate and personal struggles, and receiving prayer in those areas, is the first time I have felt what family is supposed to feel like in the church." Although some people have expressed offense that our church has broken the cultural rule of passive tolerance, the fruit — the move of the Holy Spirit in transforming lives — outweighs the cost and makes for joy-filled Kingdom work.

THE CHURCH IN THE END TIMES

This message of sin's gravity and the joyful power available to those who repent reaches its culmination in the climax of the Biblical narrative — John's book of the Revelation of the end of time. This book is meant to prepare the church for Jesus's return and reign over the world. In the first pages, Jesus writes letters to the church to show what is most important in His heart to prepare them for the Wedding Feast of the Lamb to come. He has this to say to Christians who don't take sexual integrity seriously enough:

> *I have this against you, that you tolerate that woman Jezebel, who calls herself a prophetess and is teaching and seducing my servants to practice sexual immorality and to eat food sacrificed to idols. I gave her time to repent, but she refuses to repent of her sexual immorality. Behold, I will throw her onto a sickbed, and those who commit adultery with her I will throw into great tribulation, unless they repent of her works, and I will strike her children dead. And all the churches will know that I am he who searches mind and heart, and I will give to each of you according to your works.*
> *Revelation 2:20-23*

Again, at the end of time, Jesus reveals Himself as radically challenging, not afraid of a difficult rebuke and, at the same time, radically merciful, giving the weak time to repent, desiring His church to be a pure and spotless bride, united with Him forever. Don't all prospective grooms care about what their brides do with their bodies?

It's compelling that Jesus, as He did in the gospel accounts, appeals not just to external behavior but reveals Himself as "he who searches mind and heart."[61] From Jesus's words and perspective, *how we believe,*

---

[61] Revelation 2:23

think, and feel regarding sexuality is a big deal. He promises mercy and blessing to those who will reckon with their actions, thoughts, and hearts, and He promises difficulty and a removal of blessing for Christians who refuse to participate in this purifying work in preparing for His return.

Read in its entirety, the New Testament should inspire a fearful reckoning in us as we examine our consciences and ask: have I been faithful to Jesus with my body, mind, and heart? Am I ready to stand before Him, fully exposed in body, mind, and spirit?

At the same time — and this is our hope and belief as Christians — we *do* have access to all we need for healing. We *do* have access to real transformation. That's what makes Christianity different from Judaism. We have the audacity to believe that the ways of God are no longer an external expectation but can — through the indwelling power of the Holy Spirit — be lived in both our behavior and in the deepest motivations of the heart. This journey to holiness is called sanctification, and it never ends this side of heaven. But the access to a different and better way of living and loving *is* available to us, in a way that our forefathers in the faith didn't have available to them. Because the word of God lives not outside in books but inside our hearts, we can live what Paul invited us into:

> *"Don't copy the behavior and customs of this world, but let God transform you into a new person by changing the way you think. Then you will learn to know God's will for you, which is good and pleasing and perfect"*
> Romans 12:2 NLT

The power of the uncompromised church continues today. Experiencing a church environment full of the expectation of Jesus's transforming work changed the course of my wife Jordyn's life. After sharing with her pastor's wife about her adulterous and broken relationship, Jordyn listened as this spiritual leader shared her own story of brokenness and redemption. Then Jordyn was lovingly brought into discipleship and community with this pastor's family as she navigated the difficulty of leaving her sinful relationship behind for Jesus's best for her.

The choices weren't easy. Jordyn felt her desires waver between the illicit relationship and the prospect of life without it. When the draw of true spiritual community finally outweighed the risk of leaving behind the familiarity of sin, Jordyn heard Jesus speak into her heart, "Finally! We can run!" Although far from an easy road, Jordyn was given the inspiration she needed to give everything to Jesus by a church community who had the guts to go into her broken places and call her into freedom.

Now that we have a general sense of the Biblical witness about sexuality, brokenness, redemption and sanctification, we need to look at just *how* this all works. The inability to offer reliable, logical, practical help to people struggling with their sexuality is what has led many churches to forsake Orthodoxy and adopt a watered-down version of grace that is absent from the witness of the fiery, clear-eyed New Testament writers.

With the guidance and revelation of the Holy Spirit, we will now move beyond the ideological into the gloriously messy practicals of life: brokenness, healing, and redemption for ourselves and those we love. While the first part of our study has been objective — focusing on what is true that stands apart from personal experience — now we will examine our experiences to discover why sexual integrity and gender confidence can be hard for us and how we enter into the intimacy without shame of Eden that Jesus makes available to us.

PART TWO

*The
Church's
Call*

Chapter Six

UNDERSTANDING GENDER IDENTITY & SEXUAL DEVELOPMENT

"By the principle of the incarnation the Highest is transposed into the lowest and man finds himself resurrected in every faculty of his being."

Leanne Payne

Because we believe that the Bible is true, we have unwavering faith that Jesus transforms lives and that He is eternally committed to do so. How He does that is another question. All the Bible reading I experienced in my upbringing did me little good because it wasn't paired with practical and down-to-earth application. I knew what the Bible said but had no idea how to live it out.

Thankfully, as I began to follow Jesus as an adult, He placed me in settings where I could both study God's word and also come to understand why I struggled to love and how to obtain and maintain freedom to love.[63] Those settings included counseling, support groups, and life-on-life friendships in the church. Transformation occurs when we pair the truth of the gospel with the revelation of our unique humanity and we learn to integrate spirituality into our deepest questions, hurts, and needs. One area that is unique for each of us, and that must be integrated into our spiritual lives, is our particular embodiment of gender.

---

[63] This is the explicit purpose of Comiskey's book and program *Living Waters: Restoring Relational Integrity through the Broken Body of Christ*. Much of the information in this chapter describing gender development is lifted from Chapter 10 of that book.

My friend Clint is a good example. After his father abandoned the family shortly after Clint's birth, his mother drew closer to him in an attempt to make up for his father's absence. As a result, Clint found himself modeling the more effeminate voicing and mannerisms of his mother and other female family members. After several instances of sexual abuse, Clint was sexually confused and prone to fantasizing about being a woman — anything to escape the pain of his reality.

Since Clint has entered into healing through our church community, he's been challenged and called forward specifically as a man. To watch him stand in front of a room and teach with authority and compassion on healing from abuse and trauma is remarkable indeed. He leads and he risks — he is becoming more and more comfortable in the body God gave him, and he embodies the power of God in a positively inspiring way. His growth into secure manhood mirrors his spiritual growth.

Our gender is a profound aspect of our humanity. I will never have a human experience other than a man's experience; likewise, women can never experience life outside of femininity, no matter how hard they may try. Our understanding of what it means to be human is intricately tied into our experience of our gendered bodies. Each person, however, has a unique way they view and live out the meaning of their bodies. What does it *mean* to be a man, and how do I measure up to that meaning? These are questions we must ponder in depth. Neglecting to face this reality of gender will leave us aimless and uncomfortable in our humanity.

God designed us to understand and embody our gender with great confidence through the impartation of parents, siblings, and peers. We are all born with a body, but none of us is born with an *understanding* of our body and its meaning. This understanding is imparted through our caregivers and our culture and can set us up for either deep confidence or insecurity in our given gender, depending on the truthfulness and gentleness of that impartation.

Each person's story is unique and universal at the same time. Each of us has a mother and father, but we each have a very unique experience with those two who brought us life. Each of us have caregivers and peers yet experienced them uniquely. Likewise, we each have a cultural and religious background that has shaped us powerfully. In order to understand why we handle our sexuality and our drive for intimacy differently, we must understand how we came into a sense of ourselves, as sexuality is the overflow of the self into the external world.

Recognizing each person's unique story, we must move forward with a tender realization that no "rules" define each life the same way, yet I believe we can look at a few very basic themes of our development to find where good truth and confidence were imparted into us and where confusion or lies may be affecting our process of becoming full-bodied expressions of masculinity and femininity.

As important as our experience is our *perception* of our experience and our *response* to that experience. Children are remarkably perceptive, yet they can interpret what they perceive in many ways. A few responses to our environment growing up can have life-long ramifications.

INTERNALIZATION[64]

I compare the internalizing heart to a sponge. Whatever is poured into that heart is soaked in and fills the emerging heart. One response to our caregivers and culture is to internalize the message they send us. This is exactly what many parents long for most — to see their children believe and internalize the encouragements and warnings they offer on that child's route to becoming a mature man or woman. When I tell my son that he's a leader, or I whisper in my daughter's ear that she is precious and valuable, I desire nothing more than that they would soak in those words and believe them deeply.

Just as we can internalize positive and affirming messages, we can also internalize damaging or false messages. Imagine hearing "What's wrong with you?" every day of your childhood. "Stupid." "Ugly." These statements can mark a soul and affect a young person's confidence in their ability to achieve fulfilling intimacy or to bless others powerfully.

Messages not only come through statements from parents but through other sources as well. Culture, secular or religious, sends powerful messages about what it means to be a man or woman. We hear messages such as "men shouldn't need anyone to help them" and "women always get mistreated," and we may decide that this will be our destiny, too.

---

[64] Comiskey, *Living Waters*, p. 202; Nicolosi, Shame and Attachment Loss, p. 71

Internalizing good messages about the gendered self tends to make a young man or woman confident, open to input, and equipped to navigate the many challenges en route to healthy intimacy. Conversely, internalizing damaging messages such as "something is wrong with me" or "being a man/woman means being hurt" can lead to a tendency toward addiction, isolation, or other pathology.

DETACHMENT

Internalizing is one response to the messages we hear from our environment, but it isn't the only one. Often, we hear messages, see examples, or perceive cultural norms, and, rather than allowing our hearts to absorb those influences like a sponge, we build a wall to keep the influence out. Detachment is the wall that says: "I don't want what you have to offer me."[65]

In some scenarios, detachment can be necessary and even desirable. The appropriate response to abuse or bullying is to separate oneself from the harmful situation or relationship. However, many times, vulnerable children and young adults can *perceive* a threat from a caregiver and respond by detaching from someone with whom they desperately need connection (i.e., a "good-enough" but imperfect mother or father).

Extensive damage can be done to an emerging young man or woman if he/she looks at a mother or father and declares: "I don't want to be anything like him/her." The problem with this statement is obvious: there's no one else on earth I am more like than my parents — I carry their DNA in my blood. This kind of a detachment results in a cutting off of a person from his/her very self.[66]

In taking inventory of our upbringing, we do well to avoid too much self-analysis. Instead, we should invite Holy Spirit, our wonderful counselor, to reveal significant moments of impact on our own gender development, and to reveal where He may want to speak into our experiences and responses to define new and better ones for us today. This is the very work of sanctification — to become conformed into the image of God rather than the image of our earthly brokenness. This is a grossly overgeneralized starting point in understanding gender development and insecurity, but some experiences that can be particularly significant follow.

---

[65] Nicolosi, *Shame and Attachment Loss*, p. 70-71

[66] Leanne Payne, *Crisis in Masculinity*.

EARLY LIFE AND LEARNING ATTACHMENT

As we enter the world from our mother's womb, we are utterly dependent on the care of others for life itself. God's intention during this time is for us to receive tender and attuned attention to our needs for food, cleanliness, and comfort. When these needs are met, primarily through a "good enough" birth mother, important truth gets instilled in us: *When all I have to offer are cries, dirty diapers and spit-up, I am seen, cared for and tended to, even doted upon.* This is the foundation upon which all other development grows.[67] After all, if no one cares for me, what is relationship worth?

A failure to attach to one's mother in the first two years of life can leave one with a sense of deep-seated anxiety or self-hatred.[68] The tricky thing about this wound is that none of us remembers these years. If a mother was unable to tend to our earliest needs, either through death, illness, or abandonment, we are impacted deeper than words or logic since babies at this age lack both language and logic.

Take Jordyn for example. In the hours after her birth, her lungs collapsed, and she was rushed to a hospital far from her mother. There, she recovered, often alone for the most vulnerable first weeks of her life through no fault of hers or her mothers. She obviously doesn't remember these first weeks of life (and no one could claim to know the exact impact of this time on her development), but acknowledging them has given her grace to view the deep-seated anxiety she felt as a young child and her tendency toward masturbation in the years well before puberty. Even as a girl with no understanding of why she was acting out, she intuitively came upon sexuality as a way of coping with and balancing anxiety. As she began following Jesus in her adult years, He opened doors of discipleship and prayer ministry that helped her see some connection between her struggle with sin, her emotional struggle with anxiety, and His perfect provision as God. This helped her forsake masturbation as an appropriate coping mechanism, approach God with her anxiety, and receive care and nurture from Holy Spirit where she most needed it.

---

[67] Nicolosi, *Shame and Attachment Loss*, p. 63-64.
[68] Bessel Van der Kolk, *The Body Keeps the Score*, Chapter 7

TODDLER YEARS AND THE SAME-SEX PARENT

Nothing impacts our sense of our gendered selves more than our relationship with our same-sex parent. Nothing. How he/she modeled being a man or woman, how we responded to that example, and how he/she led us into our own expression of our gender is absolutely essential.[69]

As babies become toddlers, they become obsessed with their individuality. "NO!" Is the word of these years. "No" means "I'm not the same as mommy — I'm my own person with my own desires!" Toddlers have gained a sense of their uniqueness but still lack a sense of who they actually *are*. For that, they look to role models, most importantly the same-sex parent. God has given the same-sex parent to the child in part to provide an example and mentor in the way they walk, talk, and behave as a young boy or girl.[70]

Sometimes boys can have a harder time than girls at this age because a young boy needs to turn away from his mother and learn to strengthen a bond with dad outside of his familiar care from mom. If dad is absent often, either for a job or through divorce and abandonment, another role model or mentor may step up and become a source of affirmation and encouragement. In absence of any such role model, the young boy may perceive a lack of care and may not have an easily accessible example of masculinity to which to aspire. This was Clint's story. When it came time for him to realize his boyhood, there wasn't a man around to model what that meant. Of course he wouldn't understand or feel secure as an emerging boy!

This difficult bond with a same-sex parent involves a lot of correction and encouragement, and along the way, opportunities abound for internalizing damaging messages or detaching from this parent who offers so much to the toddler's emerging sense of their gender.

In these years, I endured much verbal and physical bullying from my older brother, whom I perceived to be bonded closely with my

---

[69] Comiskey, *Living Waters*, p. 201

[70] Obviously, we all have gender influences beyond our same-sex parent. We also look to cultural stereotypes for messages about gender. When a same-sex parent isn't fully available, another mentor, family member, or peer can impart powerful paths to gender identification for better or worse. Generally speaking, the stronger a bond is with the same-sex parent, the less a young child will look to other role models, while the weaker that bond is, the stronger the influence of others in the family, peer group, or culture will be.

dad.[71] Rather than experiencing a sense of belonging with my male family members, I felt excluded from the club. My response? If they didn't want me, I didn't want them. I became averse to spending time with my father and criticized anything he tried to offer me.

THE INFLUENCE OF PEERS

As impactful as parental relationships are to our confidence and clarity, we also learn to define ourselves in relationship to our siblings and peers.[72] Especially as we enter school, we are learning not just how we express our gender in our family, but also how boys and girls act as friends. Ideally, by this point in our life, we have internalized that we belong in our family, but now we must learn to achieve satisfying same-sex friendships. A young boy or girl coming from an affirming and safe home will usually have an easier time achieving this, but a young boy or girl who has had difficulty bonding with their same-sex parent will likely see that difficulty repeated in their attempts to bond with same-sex peers.

During elementary school, girls seem to gravitate towards each other, as do boys, and they both look across the room and declare that the opposite gender "has cooties." What these kids are saying is, "You're different from me and that freaks me out," because *learning a sense of belonging with same-sex peers precedes an ability to launch into oppo-site-sex relationships.*

At this stage, some may play out false notions of being a boy or girl who "fits in." My wife, Jordyn, sought to find a sense of belonging as a girl by putting down other girls — she became a "mean girl" in response to her fears about fitting in.

In my home, I bonded quickly with my mom and sister, but never felt an ease or comfort in bonding with my dad or brother. Therefore, when I entered school, I walked, talked, and behaved in more feminine ways. I didn't feel like a girl but preferred to hang out with girls. From other boys, I experienced bullying and rejection, which deepened my

---

[71] In our adult years, my brother has genuinely repented of his treatment toward me in our adolescence, and we enjoy a close relationship today. As I share about some pain he caused in my early years, I would be remiss to exclude the great joy and blessing he has brought to my life in the years since. Truly, our brotherhood serves as an example of God's redeeming and restoring power.
[72] Nicolosi, *Shame and Attachment Loss*, p. 103

feeling that something was different and wrong about me. I felt there must be a reason that the boys liked each other but not me.

CREATING AN IDENTITY

As puberty hits, a dramatic influx of sex hormones forces us to navigate our new, powerful desires for the kids who formerly felt intimidatingly different. At this point in life, we take all the messages and relationships that we have internalized and begin to stumble into an adult "self" we project into the world.[73]

As teens, most of us are averse to input from mom and dad, but at this juncture, we especially need the voice of a father to give us clarity and definition as an emerging adult. Young women need fathers who will protect them and bless their dignity and beauty as they risk giving themselves in relationship. Young men need fathers to model how to pursue and honor women and to help equip them to do so. All teens need their parents to give them an understanding of the changes happening to their bodies and spirits during puberty and direction to turn those desires into a source of honor and blessing to the world. In short, teens have to learn to see a world beyond immediate thrills and to fashion a public identity while learning to tend to the needs of others beyond themselves.

IDENTITY IS A PROCESS

All the stages of "becoming" men and women build on the ones before. Thus, kids from healthy families tend to make friends easily, steer clear of unhealthy relationships and addictive behaviors, and head more easily into stable and honoring romantic relationships leading to marriage.

On the other hand, teens who have had more challenges before puberty tend to have difficulty forming a secure identity to present to the world. They may freeze up at the prospect of romance and tend more towards isolation. They may be vulnerable to the comfort, thrill, and accompanying shame of pornography. They may be more vulnerable to fashioning a "gay" or "trans-" identity to make sense of the isolation and rejection they've experienced.

---

[73] Nicolosi, *Shame and Attachment Loss*, p. 120-124.

None of us are reduced to easy equations. Sometimes people come from terrible family environments, yet somehow find a strong sense of confidence and security. Conversely, many people grow up in stable and "healthy enough" homes, yet find difficulty later in securing good friendships or steering clear of unhealthy sexual or relational patterns.

Even teens who are best set up for success have many challenges to navigate on the road to becoming healthy adults, and we all have a sinful nature that seeks to keep us bound to sin and shame. Sexual sin is an equal-opportunity offender, infecting both the most privileged and most vulnerable. In fact, the chemical power of sexual release means that at a very physical level, masturbation and pornography can quickly alter the neural pathways of the brain, rendering addiction and shame into a psyche that could otherwise be set up for great relational success.

Thus, we see the Biblical warning play out in everyday life: "The one who sins sexually sins against his own body,"[74] and we live in the duality of being both sinners and those sinned against by others whom God intended to be consistent sources of care, concern, and development. The purpose of examining early relationships, therefore, isn't to attach blame, but rather to grow in an understanding of deeply rooted belief systems that affect adult emotions and behavior.

EFFECTS OF SILENCE

One obstacle for many teens in Christian homes is the prudery and silence from parents regarding puberty and sexuality. When I teach on sexuality in church settings, I usually ask the group how many people had parents who gave extensive input and discussion about their bodies, gender, and sexuality. In rooms of 50-100 adults, usually one to five express having received this helpful sex education from their parents. I am left to assume many Christian teenagers are left to themselves to navigate puberty, which is tragic. It's not surprising, then, that many of us have reached bad conclusions about what it means to be a man or woman, created for intimacy and relationship.

---

[74] 1 Corinthians 6:18

CREATING A NARRATIVE

For the first part of my life, my narrative was all too familiar. As I already mentioned, I felt a deep antipathy toward my dad from an early age. I didn't have words for the disconnection I felt and could honestly look at others and say I had a wonderful Christian family. In truth, I did experience a wonderful Christian family, but I failed to experience the kind of specific care and concern that would help secure within me a sense of strength, security, and courage in the face of obstacles. In short, I failed to receive a sense of meaning behind my masculinity.

Again, I had no language around this need or lack for many years. All I knew was that I disliked my dad, felt unsafe around my brother's bullying, and felt like I never fit in with the other boys at school or church. I had a few boys who were life-long friends and who treated me very kindly, but I always wondered if they *really* liked me, or just pitied me (perceptions that influenced my interpretation of reality).

As puberty hit, so did waves of sexual attraction toward my male friends, along with a lot of shame and a deep sense that something was wrong with me. And, at that point, without trustworthy wisdom or help, I began to create a narrative according to my feelings.

My first narrative involved the deception that I could pray a magical prayer and God would "zap" away my inconvenient same-sex attraction if He was truly faithful and powerful. I chose to become dependent on sexual fantasy and masturbation because it was the only way I could escape my feelings of isolation and hiddenness and my fear of rejection. While choosing this addiction, I would beg God to change me and wonder why He wasn't changing me. I presented an image to the world in high school of a smart, successful leader and Christian, but on the inside, I wasn't so sure of this narrative. I lacked *integrity*, a unified sense of myself both alone and in public, where the outside matched my inner world.

In college, I tried a different narrative. I believed my same-sex attraction was never going to change; therefore, God either didn't care, or didn't have the right to care, if He even existed. I believed that my feelings of isolation and rejection all stemmed from my failure to accept and embrace my homosexuality, so my pursuit of fulfillment consisted of finding the right man to cause me to feel love and to feel loved, to inspire faithfulness and consistency in me. When the right guy never came along, I had permission to do whatever I wanted to feel fulfilled. When I felt the right guy was near, I would do anything and everything to secure that he liked me. I believed I had no family problems — my feelings were the result and evidence of my need for homosexual sex.

The problem with this narrative is that it didn't account for the guilt and shame I still felt when no one was looking, and it put me outside of accountability toward anyone else. During this time, when I felt guilt and shame, I attributed those feelings to my conservative upbringing. Therefore, no one was allowed to tell me my behavior was inappropriate, so no one could help alleviate the shame and fear of exposure I continued to experience.

I find this is what we do when we have feelings and experiences we don't understand. We often seek to make sense of them on our own, outside of God's word or the counsel of wise mentors or church covering. Once we've constructed our narrative, it can be very hard for anyone to question or doubt that narrative without us perceiving that they are questioning or doubting our very self.

Once I submitted my life to Jesus's ways and Word, He challenged me to look at how I came into my sense of myself and my masculinity. He allowed me to question why I felt so inadequate as a man and opened me to the possibility of my insecurities and personhood being influenced by my formative relationships with family and friends. I began to understand that I had both sinned greatly and been greatly sinned against. I began to understand that I had been deprived of deep needs for affirmation and affection, and I began to understand that God wanted to meet those needs in clean, non-sexual ways.

Re-defining my narrative with God's Word meant aligning with central Biblical truths and using Biblical language to describe my experiences. Rather than "being gay," I was experiencing temptation toward perversion and lust. Rather than blaming a "dysfunctional" parent, I came to regard my family system as one in which all had sinned and fallen short of showing me God's glory. I needed help from God, both to strengthen me to reject temptation toward lust and immorality and to fill in the pieces of my masculinity and personhood that had felt lacking for my entire life. My challenge was to trust God to restore what I could never change, while embracing the things that only I could change: my responses to my pain & insecurity and my choices of how to treat and lead my own mind and body. I found that submitting my narrative to the universal truth revealed by God in Scripture and prayer opened up a big horizon for my life as well as provided ample opportunity to examine the parts of my heart that still need His healing and leadership.

CONTINUING TO BECOME WHOLE

Each person's upbringing is unique, and each of us responded differently to the good and bad influences around us. We chose what to let in and what to push away. We internalized messages about our gender and our capacity or desire to fulfill the calling our gender gives us. For some, looking back brings mostly warm feelings of home, mixed with some regret over mistakes made later in life. For others, looking back is a painful reminder of so much that went wrong. Some wounds have brought a complete lack of clarity: "Who am I? What was I made for?"

God has described Himself as "merciful and gracious, slow to anger and abounding in lovingkindness and truth."[75] So while we look to God's Word for the truth regarding our calling and our purpose, we can also have confidence that He understands why living that Word is so difficult for us, for reasons both spiritual and also very practical stemming from our most basic family relationships.

Again, no one's life or upbringing is a linear, "one plus one makes two" experience. We are complicated creatures living in a fallen world. More than that, however, we who follow Jesus have the experience of being "born again, not of corruptible seed but of incorruptible."[76] It stands to reason that with a new birth comes a new upbringing, a renewal in our process of becoming formed into the likeness of God in a way unique to us yet true to the Biblical narrative of gender.

No matter how numerous our challenges and wounds, God has offered to become father, mother, brother and friend to us, to "restore the devastations of many generations"[77] and to "rescue us from the empty way of life handed down to us by our forefathers."[78]

Every person's need is for someone to save us and restore us into our created potential. Every Christian's hope is that Holy Spirit will

---

[75] Exodus 34:6
[76] 1 Peter 1:23
[77] Isaiah 61:4
[78] 1 Peter 1:18

give us all we need on our journey to becoming truthful bearers of God's image and love. Our hope is actualized as God uses the power of Holy Spirit, the support of the church body, and the disciplines of the spiritual life to grow us up into mature sons and daughters of the Most High God.

Chapter Seven

PARTICIPATION
IN LOVE

"And you show that you are a letter from Christ...written not with ink
but with the Spirit of the Living God. It is not carved on tablets of stone
but on tablets of human hearts."

2 Corinthians 3:3

It is my earnest prayer that, as you've read the previous chapters of this book and have seen all God has intended for us as His children, a desire has stirred within you to enter more fully into purity, love, and generosity. But how do we do that, practically? Through participation in the disciplines of Christian spirituality, we can overcome broken ways of relating and live in lasting freedom.

For over a decade now, I have directed my life to enter more fully into Christ's love and to offer that to those closest to me without the impurities of my own lust or judgments. I haven't been perfect, but in the decade of giving all of myself to this search, I can tell you some themes I've discovered – some things that have worked for me that will hopefully be helpful for you. In addition, I've spent countless hours with other men and women who are participating in the work of redeeming their sexuality and relationships. I'll be drawing from their beautiful stories and how I've seen grace work practically *in* and *through* them.

Before we look at some important elements of purity and whole-ness in our intimate relationships, it's important to note that walking with Jesus isn't a formula, it's obedience to a person. I've listed these steps in an order I find to be true regarding importance; ultimately, we follow not man-made laws but God as He directs us.

STEP ONE: SURRENDER

In our search for freedom and wholeness, although so easily said and so difficult to live, there's no substitute for completely surrendering our hopes, dreams, and desires to Jesus, thereby making Him the true Master over our lives.[79] *He* gets to define how our needs for love get met. *He* gets to define what is true love and what is destructive infatuation. *He* gets to define if I'm trustworthy enough to have a smartphone. *He* gets to define if my motivations are pure or impure. It may seem like a given, yet there's not an issue more critical than this: those who will submit to Jesus's higher ways in the moments when it feels most costly find freedom. Those who hold on to preconceived notions or relational dreams and try to get Jesus to go along with them stay stuck. It's as simple as that.

For those with long-standing addictive patterns or gender identity conflicts that date back to earliest childhood memories, this is no small matter. When I fell down on the floor of my New York City apartment and said, "OK, Jesus, I'm yours if you'll take me — whatever that means for me," every hunger for intimacy I had experienced had been same-sex directed. I had felt gay my entire life, and my desire for that kind of completion was insatiable. In the moment I surrendered my future to Jesus, I didn't know if that meant I could stay gay-identified or not. I didn't know if it would mean a life of extreme loneliness — I thought it probably would. I didn't care. Something had shifted in me, a desire greater than happiness had emerged. What mattered became being with Jesus and being aligned with His best for me. Not my happiness. Not my experience of love. My one desire was to be upright in His eyes.

As disciples of Jesus, this must be our one desire, now and all the days of our life. Now, as a husband and father of a growing family, I see every day the temptation to "desire other things" such as wealth, entertainment, popularity, significance. I see and feel the pull of the world's

---

[79] This way of life was taught to me by Stephen H. Black who describes this lifestyle in his book *Freedom Realized*, Chapter 6 "Coram Deo".

promise of visceral, immediate thrills, and the temptation to shuck off responsibility to pursue my own pleasure. In desperate prayer, I often go back to the moment when I gave my life to Jesus. I don't belong to myself anymore; therefore, I no longer have the right to think independently of the wisdom and counsel of God. This has absolutely become my place of joy and has opened a wider horizon for my life than I ever would have imagined. But in the moments of surrender, the road that leads to life always feels narrow indeed.

Nearly every person I have had the privilege of walking in close relationship with has had to face this core question of centrality – the essential battle between the life centered around the self and its desires and the life centered around the sovereignty and supremacy of Jesus. I remember a small group meeting in which my friend Keith shared about a long-standing pattern of viewing illicit images and videos when he couldn't sleep at night. He had seen the pattern for months but resisted setting strong boundaries with his technology — he felt he would do that if the problem "got bad enough" but didn't see the need currently. The group challenged him to think about exactly how bad the problem needed to get before he prioritized his integrity before God over his smartphone convenience. He surrendered his rights before God and committed to prioritize his character above convenience. A month or so later he shared that he'd been sober since making that commitment. A few years later I stood with him on his wedding day as he gave himself as a husband with no secrets and proven, trustworthy character.

I also think about my friend Kristen, who rejected her desire to hold onto her reputation and instead came boldly into the light with our church regarding her sexual addiction. Her motivation wasn't neces- sarily an internal drive to do better; rather, in prayer one day she heard Jesus clearly ask her to begin to bring this area of her life into the open. As a female and one who had served as a leader in our church, this took no small amount of courage. But Kristen decided that looking good mattered less to her than becoming good — obeying Jesus and begin- ning to stand in sobriety and face abuse and trauma that had left her vulnerable to addiction. She's now been sober for years and has walked many other women out of sexual addiction through the power of her testimony and boldness in calling more women to come forward into freedom.

Of course, our choice to say "yes" to Jesus also necessitates an option to say "no" to Him, to keep trying to find justification and peace on our own. Many turn the conflict within them outward, taking out their anger or desire for acceptance on others, demanding a kind of recognition and permission to live how they want from everyone around them. Most of us know people who are stuck here, and they are often very challenging to live in relationship with because they cannot receive love and acceptance unless it's accompanied by an agreement with all of their life decisions and beliefs.

A few years ago, I met with an individual who was born a man but had struggled for years with a feeling that he was a woman trapped in a man's body. His gender dysphoria had been evident for many years. He wore women's clothes and had undergone hormone therapy. His confusion had led to an instability in his life overall — he couldn't seem to hold a job and had been homeless for years. But he came to our church regularly on Sunday mornings. He'd sit in the back, but he'd come.

This man had been loved by many in our church who would give him money and time as they invested in hearing his story and praying with him in his pain. As years passed, this man kept attending our church, but he progressively became more and more feminized, wearing wigs and makeup that looked clownish and, unfortunately, resulted in many people backing away — his appearance had become frightful. It angered me that Satan was wanting to rob this soul of his basic dignity. I knew he needed healthy connection but also knew that the wigs and make-up were functioning as a type of wall to keep people from really being able to get close.

I asked for some time to speak with this seeker. I expressed my love for and belief in him and my desire to see him experience the fullness of the life and love of Christ. I asked him how he felt in relationship to Jesus. Did he feel nearer to Jesus now than he did years ago when he began attending our church? His response was, "I don't know, Andrew. I don't smoke. I don't drink. I don't use people or judge people like I see other people doing. I just have this one thing of... I don't know... the way I am. And I feel like I just have to be okay with that." I asked him if he believed Jesus was okay with his decisions. He replied, "Again, I'm not drinking or getting wasted. There's a lot I'm not doing wrong. So, I think Jesus sees that... I just don't know." He told me many stories of other Christians he knew that were living in sin and asked why his should be such a big deal.

I commended him for all the ways he was trying to do what's right. I sought to gently point out to him that, as Christians, we never want to camp out on what makes us better than other Christians, but rather focus on where Jesus is asking us to grow and become more like Him. Did he want to become more like Jesus, or did he want to become more permissive with the desires he knew were outside of Jesus's best for him? He responded by pointing out how he could tell by the way people looked at him that they judged his wig and make-up. He wanted to feel loved, but sometimes he felt judged. Was it okay for them to judge?

Again, I asked him to set aside his questions regarding what was okay for other people and asked if his conscience was clean regarding his own choices. This man, in such a vulnerable scenario, had the courage to share that he knew that his choices regarding his gender confusion — the costumes and wigs — were making it difficult to find healthy connection with people. He courageously told me he knew that his appearance was a wall he was putting up to keep people away, even though he knew that wall was only hurting himself.

I expressed the same thing I express to everyone at our church — that Jesus always has more for us than we could hope or imagine. But He allows us to choose. I expressed that our church would always strive to love him and would also always point him to become more aligned with Jesus, more like Him. Did he want to follow Jesus and become more like him?

Abruptly, this man ended our meeting and told me he needed to leave. I grieved over his response. I was tempted to doubt myself. I asked myself and the Lord if I had been too forward, forcing too much on him.

Then I remembered Jesus's invitation to the rich young ruler[80] — a man who wanted to be justified through all the things he was doing right. Jesus didn't shy away from asking the young man to follow Him in still greater ways. Jesus wanted him to move forward with Him. And the man walked away. Jesus grieves when we reject the narrow way that leads to life, but He never shies away from inviting us, no matter our response.

---

[80] Mark 10:17-27

For those who do commit to Jesus, baptism becomes a sign of our vow to God — the public death of the bodily life separated from Holy Spirit, and the public birth of a life wedded, joined, and united with Holy Spirit. Baptism became for me a line in the sand — a moment which I couldn't deny, in which I had given up my own life and assumed the call to carry the Divine Life of God inside my body, for better or for worse. It has turned out to be so very much for the better.

STEP TWO: GET HONEST

Apart from refusing to surrender to Jesus's invitation, perhaps our greatest hindrance to freedom is unconfessed sin. Sin thrives in secrecy — this is what the Bible calls walking in darkness. Many things might be lurking in darkness, either good or bad — but the point is that what is in darkness is unseen and unknown by others.[81]

If I turn the lights on in a room in my house, it doesn't make the room clean, but it lets me see what needs to be cleaned up. So it is with confession. What's more, we have the promise that as we come into the light, Jesus will clean in us what we cannot clean by ourselves. But essential to this exchange is coming into the light with other Christians:

> *"If we say we have fellowship with Him yet walk in the darkness, we lie and do not practice the truth. But if we walk in the light as He is in the light, we have fellowship with one another and the blood of Jesus His son cleanses us from all sin"*
> *1 John 1:7*

Did you notice what John said we would get by honestly exposing our sin? *Fellowship.* It's the place where, married or single, we can all find an answer to our longing for intimacy. When we become fully known, we begin to experience what Adam and Eve experienced: nakedness and exposure, but with the absence of shame. Shame is removed through connection.

Some of you may contend that you have friendships and function inside the church just fine, thank you, without exposing all the grievous sins of your past. I've even heard many Christians use religious language

---

[81] For more on confession and living honestly, see Comiskey, *Living Waters*, Chapter 6

to justify staying in the dark, contending that Jesus alone forgives, so Jesus alone needs to know of their sin or their past. It is true that Jesus alone is the one who imparts forgiveness, but it's also true that Jesus has chosen His church to be the location for forgiveness to be imparted. While privately (read: secretly) confessing your sins to Jesus may well be sufficient for eternal pardon, what remains is an underlying fear that if someone else really knew you, really knew what you've done, they would think differently of you. That stronghold of shame can only die when every shameful sin we have chosen has come into the light where we can receive forgiveness and acceptance from a member of the Body.

James has a prescription for us as well: "Confess your sins to one another and pray for one another, so that you may be healed" (James 5:16). This is a simple prescription similar to one a doctor would give a sick patient. You want to know healing from strongholds of confusion, addiction, bad and poor relationships? Find another member or members of the church and confess your sins to them. Receive their prayer and receive the forgiveness of Jesus through this trusted, "safe-enough" person. Look in their eyes and receive a glimpse of the love and forgiveness of Jesus. And feel what it's like to be fully seen, fully known, fully accepted, and fully loved.

Many months after I'd left New York City and was seeking to walk with Jesus and reject homosexual activity, I found myself lonely. Most of the friends I had shared the previous five years with had ceased friendship with me as a result of the spiritual (and many times immature) zealotry I'd adopted. I had left behind friends who could only recognize and relate to me as a gay man, but I hadn't had time to develop similarly intimate relationships with healthy Christians. I was making relational inroads, though, with a small group of young men who were following Jesus wholeheartedly. I was grateful for them, but I had no desire to let any of them in on my intense loneliness and its result— a fantasy-world in which I wondered what it would be like to go back to the life I had left behind.

I began a book study with these men — a book which included a section on the confession of sin. As we intellectually discussed confession, one guy took the bold step to actually open up about an area of sin by which he felt bound. I listened and prayed, but I wasn't ready to open up quite yet.

A few weeks later, I found myself wondering further what my life would be like if I went back to New York and forgot about my foray into Christianity. I knew I needed the strength of another believer to help me in my weakness, but I was terrified that opening up to a guy who seemed to be much more mature would mean I'd be judged, rejected, or condescended. I believed that, after a few months of walking with Jesus, I shouldn't have still been struggling with the same old things. However, more than my fear, I desired freedom from these oppressive thoughts.

I wrote down my confession because I didn't want to doctor it up to make myself look better in the moment of vulnerability. I asked one of these young men to meet and pray with me, and I read him (rather monotonously & emotionlessly) my confession of fantasy and considering leaving Jesus behind. After reading it out loud, I looked up at my friend. He was crying. He told me his heart broke for me as he saw the struggle I was under and the reality of all I'd left behind. He prayed that my soul would be strengthened, and he asked how he could better support me.

In that moment, the area of struggle that I thought would get me judged and condemned was the very gateway to my feeling a sense of healthy intimacy, fellowship, and camaraderie that I'd never felt with another man. I felt like he *got* it, that he could *feel* what I felt and love me there. Whereas many in my gay community could understand my past but couldn't accept where I was heading, a man with the mark of Jesus on his life could look into my past and present, and while accepting all that mess, could remind me who I was in Jesus's eyes and encourage me in the path ahead. That scary step opened a new rhythm in my life of quickly exposing sin, and eventually quickly exposing even the temptation to sin. The more quickly we "expose the deeds of darkness,"[82] the more quickly light comes in that shows us the way forward with Jesus.

I've seen countless men and women transform from being emotionally shutdown to being joyfully, spiritually alive by exposing difficult areas of unconfessed sin. One man came to me struggling with anger issues toward his wife and children. Later, he confessed to committing sexually predatory behavior toward some women during his college

---

[82] Ephesians 5:11

years, and I could tell as he shared that he would have rather curled up in a ball and died. As we prayed, I asked him to listen to what Jesus was saying to him about his past sins. He said, "Jesus told me it's all washed away," but as he said it, sobs overtook his body as he *experienced* the reality of forgiveness for the first time. That day, he agreed to forgive himself and stop holding himself captive to the shame of his past. As a result, the next time we met he testified of the deeper connection, love, and acceptance he felt toward his family. As he received forgiveness in his depths, he could accept his family for who they were without judging them with the judgment he had internalized for himself. That is the power of confessing sin.

My wife ministered to a woman who was struggling with a cyclically immoral relationship. This woman knew that answering a certain man's phone calls would always result in a moral failure, yet she felt powerless to say no to him. After confessing this to her small group, she returned the next week with a new story. This same man had called her again, and she felt the desire to connect with him. However, she then remembered the love she had received from the women in her small group. She remembered her confession and realized she didn't want to go back confessing the same failure again. So, rather than accepting a perverted intimacy, she came back to a group of friends and celebrated victory with them. What's more, other women in the group began to set stronger boundaries in their lives, inspired by the confession and resulting strength from their friend.

We have a choice when it comes to confession. Our freedom will parallel our level of honesty. While I've seen the power of deep confession many times, I've also seen the impotence of socially-acceptable, vague confession. Certain confessions are easier than others, and often deep, dark motives of the heart are excruciating to admit. It is easier to communicate in ways that skirt the pain of confession, but the result is a soul that is still in bondage to shame, still vulnerable to going to back to the same darkness again. Sin thrives in secrecy. Sexual sin and proclivities thrive in the dark, where our enemy can torture us with condemning statements like "You're so perverted. No one else would think to want that." Or, "You'll never change or be free." In love, Holy Spirit spurs us into sharing these depths with others, and in power,

He activates us to reject and renounce the condemning statements of despair, and to move toward life.

Confession is a kind of death. A death of the socially-recognized saint. A death of the "good" Christian other people think we are.[83] Before another person, we must expose the darkness we choose. In doing so, however, we are opened up to a resurrection: a new kind of life, lived in the light, supported by the community of faith.

STEP THREE: ESTABLISH BOUNDARIES

I've never seen anyone become free from sexual or relational sin without instating some healthy boundaries.[84] However, the suggestion of boundaries around internet usage or relationships often results in extreme emotional reactions. "I can't live without my smartphone — no, really, I couldn't perform my job without 24/7 access to any website out there." Sometimes we resist the very provision from God given to protect us from freedoms we aren't ready to handle.

I have a young son, and portions of our home are off-limits to him. We give him access to many things, yet I wouldn't dream of putting sharp knives within his reach. Why? It's not because knives are inherently evil. I know and fully believe that, one day, my son will learn to wield a knife safely in a way that will be very useful to him. He's just not ready for that yet. Right now, a knife in his hand would be no more than a ticket to the ER.

In the same way, those struggling with a pornography addiction must soberly ask themselves, "Am I really ready for unhindered access to the internet?" Those struggling with an illicit relationship must ask, "Am I really ready to engage with this person without crossing sexual boundary lines?"[85]

For our post-post-modern generation, boundaries are seen as nothing more than restrictions. Yet Paul strongly exhorts us to think soberly about what temptation we're ready to withstand.

"Therefore, let he who thinks he stands take heed lest he fall. For no temptation has seized you except what is common to man,

---

[83] Comiskey, *Living Waters*, p. 109
[84] Black, *Freedom Realized*, p. 99
[85] Comiskey, *Living Waters*, p. 137

and God is gracious, and with the temptation will provide a way out."

1 Corinthians 10:13

Did you catch that? God's heart is to provide a way out for us. He knows our weakness and understands our propensity to compromise the love we truly want to fight for, so He provides a way of escape. The way of escape, however, is set up when, still feeling strong, we "take heed lest we fall". We set up boundaries while we think we're doing okay so that, at our worst moments, we can escape the enticement of the enemy of love.

Remember the conversation I had with my Christian friend in which I confessed an ongoing temptation to go back into homosexuality rather than walk the narrow road with Christ? Well, that conversation forced me into some responsibility. The awareness that I was still vulnerable to the voices of others to define me meant that I needed to set up healthy boundaries in the relationships in which I had adopted a gay identity. A wise counselor told me that I needed to "establish the standard of the cross" in these friendships. To me, this meant that my friends who had known me as "gay" needed to hear from me that I was no longer identifying myself that way. I needed to express that I was identifying myself with Jesus instead, and was setting my life up to follow Him in every area and decision. That meant leaving homosexual activity, identity, and social life behind. I wasn't going to gay bars anymore. I wasn't going to commiserate with them about the ups and downs of their homosexual pursuits — I simply wasn't strong enough for that at the time.

I wish I could say those "boundary" conversations were peaceful and respectful. The truth is, I didn't communicate those boundaries perfectly or even very well. And my gay-affirming friends had no idea how to support me in such radical, politically incorrect choices. So those conversations were difficult, to say the least. Painful. Clarifying. I lost a whole set of relationships that I thought would be lifelong. It became clear that those individuals could and would only see me as a gay man living repressed and closeted, and I would only see them as people needing Jesus. Those two viewpoints were simply irreconcilable.

The lonely period of grief that followed was bearable only because I was simultaneously doing the work of developing healthy intimacy within a Christian community. Jesus provided miraculously. The same week that many of these painful boundary conversations occurred happened to be a Holy Week my Christian community was observing. This group of friends had decided to camp out for the week to foster deeper connection while celebrating the deliverance of Jesus. Every night I was tempted to stay at home and bemoan the loss of my relationships. But night after night, as I showed up, Jesus made a way for me to connect meaningfully with this group of friends, and by the end of the week, I felt like I was one of them — not the outsider trying to get in, but having equal footing. Mutual relationship. I needed to lose friendships that were taking my time and leading to confusion in order to have the space for new relationships that could affirm my identity in Christ.

Setting boundaries is hard. It feels restrictive. And, underlying any choice to put a boundary in place lies a fear that we'll find a way around it. Most men I have ministered to who resist setting internet boundaries don't resist them as much for their inconvenience as they resist out of a fear that they will find the loophole. Their true fear is *failure*. It's easier to blame the big bad internet for our moral failures than it is to face the compulsive grasping of our sin nature. But face it we must.

This is why confession and boundary-setting must go hand-in-hand. Without boundaries, we confess the same moral failure over and over again, without seeing transformation, wondering why we seem set up for failure in Christianity. With boundaries in place, we can face the darkness of our heart with a brother or sister in Christ. Without the destructive items available to attach to, we're forced to develop connection and relationship to fill in the gap. Then, as we receive healing, connection, and prayer, our hearts are gradually transformed to desire the "narrow road that leads to life" more than easy, destructive attachments.

ATTACHMENT FREE

God created our bodies to seal in the spirituality of marital commitment hormonally. Scientists have found that the act of sex releases the hormone oxytocin. When sexual connection happens between a man and wife, oxytocin is released in the body and seals in the memory of intimacy, tying two hearts and minds together permanently. It's a beautiful reality of two becoming one. (The same hormone later signals mothers in labor to contract their reproductive parts and is again released to serve as a bonding element when mothers nurse their newborns!) Unfortunately, the same chemical and spiritual reality happens when a sexual connection isn't so pure.[86] That explains why men and women who have crossed sexual boundary lines are haunted by oppressive memories or attractions to those they have engaged with intimately. If our bodies were created for this sealing of sexual unity, what hope is there for freedom when this has been perverted? How can we move forward?

One key lies in healing prayer. Paul lays the groundwork for this in 1 Corinthians 5:16-17: "Don't you realize that if a man joins himself to a prostitute, he becomes one body with her? For the Scriptures say, 'The two are united into one.' But the person who is joined to the Lord is one spirit with him."

Basic Christian doctrine holds that a connection with God *must* be stronger than connection with a mere human. When united with Jesus in a spiritual communion, former destructive commitments we've made with our bodies can be broken through the authority of Jesus. This can look quite practical in prayer.

When I've felt the impact of my immoral choices with others through powerful memories or familiar temptation, I have learned to assert this freedom from unholy sexual ties. While united with Jesus in prayer, I assert His authority and invite Him to be the boundary between my mind, heart, and body and the spirit of the one with whom I crossed boundaries. I invoke the power of the death and resurrection of Jesus to kill the power of memories of dead sin and to awaken resurrection strength to stand in purity and within healthy boundary lines. I then thank Him for setting me free, and I choose to move on with my day — I refuse to let my mind and heart be harassed by memories of powerless sin.

Assertive, spiritually-authoritative prayers are essential for a victorious Christian life, and they should be prayed regularly as we learn to

---

[86] Leanne Payne, *The Healing Presence*, p. 232ff

fight with strength and resolve. Our western culture prefers prayer life to be quiet, contemplative, and personal, and indeed, there is a lot to be said for quiet and contemplative prayer. But winning a war takes more than sweet thoughts and devotional emotions. Rather, we use Scripture and the power of Holy Spirit to speak truth and disagree with lies.

For example, when I feel a desire to look lustfully or relate flirtatiously with someone, I firmly (if in public, maybe quietly, yet firmly) state, "I disagree and renounce a spirit of lust and seduction, and I command it to go away from me in Jesus name." I then thank God for giving me "all I need for life and godliness," thank Him for the family He has called me to remain faithful to, and I go about my day in peace. There have been times, especially early on in my life in God, when I had to pray that way extremely often. Over the years, the fight has become easier as I have gained strength and authority in my spiritual life. God gives us the strength we need and prayers to assert when we need them.

RENOUNCING DEMONIC INFLUENCE

We cannot talk about Christian healing and sanctification without addressing the spirit realm, where our real battle is waged.[87] Even if we confess past and current sin and examine our family and peer influences in counseling, we will always live in a world involving the influence of demons.

This is a thoroughly Biblical worldview and essential to resolving root issues related to sexual and relational obstacles. Think about it: if human relationships are what show the world the way God loves, what will Satan activate his demonic forces to attack most? In his masterwork *The End of the Affair*, Graham Greene, a Catholic, wrote from the perspective of an atheist novelist who experiences disappointment in human love:

"I can imagine that if there existed a God who loved, the devil would be driven to destroy even the weakest, the most faulty imitation of that love. Wouldn't he be afraid that the habit of love might grow, and wouldn't he try to trap us all into being traitors, into helping him extinguish love? If there is a God who uses us and makes his saints out of such material as we are, the devil too may have his ambitions."

---

[87] Ephesians 6:12

We must fight spiritual battles of isolation, depression, lust, and perversion with spiritual weapons if we want to live victorious lives. Physical weapons and relationship-building tools will only go so far.

I have heard some assert that demons cannot influence believers because we are sealed with the Holy Spirit. While this sounds nice, my reading of the book of Ephesians, particularly Chapter 6, leads me to expect that the armor of God, necessary to win spiritual battles, was necessary for the believing church in Ephesus that Paul was addressing. Why would the Bible tell unbelievers to engage in spiritual warfare? It is the believer who has made Satan his enemy and who must, therefore, be ready to engage in the battle at hand.

While some assert that because we live in a fallen world we will always be subject to sinful proclivities, I also believe that the Holy Spirit's regenerating work in our lives means that we can truly walk in ever-increasing levels of clarity in our minds and hearts.

Here's how we can start:

1. In prayer, ask Holy Spirit to reveal to you where demonic influence has been given permission in your life.[89] If you've noticed cyclical patterns attached to lust, unforgiveness, fear, manipulation, or perversion, know that your choices have given the enemy permission to establish ground in your heart. Simply confess your participation in whichever specific influence you've been affected by, and then stand in your greater authority in Christ and renounce all agreement and participation. Command lust (or whatever your proclivity may be) to leave your thoughts and feelings and ask Jesus what He wants to give you to replace that unclean spirit.[90] We don't need to dialogue with demons when we feel familiar oppressive thoughts. We simply take the sword of the Spirit and command the enemy to flee.[91]

2. Take inventory of your family of origin. In prayer, ask Jesus to show you any demonic influence that was given permission to exist by your parents and grandparents. While no curse can pass through the cross,[92] we can and must assert this truthful authority in prayer.

---

[89] Several resources exist to assist in discerning demonic entry and deliverance. Try Geri McGhee's *Clearing the Land: Preparing for Deliverance*, or one of several books by Neil Anderson.

[90] Matthew 12:43-44

[91] James 4:7

[92] Galatians 3:13

When demonic influences like abuse, addiction, or divorce have been given ground in a family, they no longer need permission to be there — they function like squatters who live in a land (or, in this case, the spiritual territory of your heart) illegally. Jesus has given us the legal eviction papers; now, in His name, we must serve the eviction notice to the enemy. In prayer, renounce each area of historic influence from your family and thankfully receive the new inheritance Jesus has given you. You'll have new eyes to see your "tendencies" as simply nagging remnants of old family patterns that can be broken and overcome by the Holy Spirit inside of you.

3. Behind every demonic stronghold is a lie that makes us believe we need what the enemy has to offer us. For example, I participated in a seductive spirit for years, finding as many men as possible to engage with me sexually. Underneath this demonic participation was a lie that a sexual encounter would make me feel more wanted. The truth was that I was already radically desired and wanted by Jesus, and no man could replace my need to receive His love; on the contrary, sexual sin was just making me feel worthless. While I needed to renounce my participation with seduction, I also needed to allow Jesus to speak truth into my heart. So, after recognizing and renouncing demonic participation, ask Jesus to show you what lie led to that open door. In prayer, renounce your agreement with that lie. Then ask Jesus what the truth is. In prayer, audibly speak that truth over your soul and believe that it is setting health and peace in place — for "life and death is in the power of the tongue" (Proverbs 18:21). Jesus is the truth, so He loves revealing truth, and that truth really does set us free.[93]

SEEKING RECONCILIATION

While standing in the power of prayer, we must also ask ourselves if our sexual sin resulted in harm coming to the one with whom we sinned. If we truly believe that "the wages of sin is death,"[94] we must then acknowledge that our sexual sin has wrought a kind of death in those whom we have used for the fulfillment of our own lust. It matters not who initiated or complied willingly, but rather that I have made

---

[93] John 8:32
[94] Romans 6:23

choices with *my* body that infected someone else with *my* sin.[95]   In such cases, with much covering from safe Christian friends and/or pastors, I believe forgiveness should be sought, not only from God, but also from those affected by our sins. This might mean confessing to a parent or roommate your impure use of their computer. This might mean prudently contacting old lovers and asking forgiveness for participating in a sinful activity that led to their spiritual and physical defilement. When I contacted previous lovers, alongside a trusted Christian counselor, I'd say something like this:

"Hi Stuart. I know it's been awhile since we've talked, but I have given my life to follow Jesus, and I believe He would want me to ask for forgiveness from you. When we involved ourselves sexually, I didn't realize it at the time, but I was using you and not treating you with the dignity and respect you deserve. I used your body for my purposes and that's so wrong. I know you might see things differently, but would you forgive me for my sexual involvement with you? I want you to be free from the consequences of my bad choices."

Often my exes had no idea how to respond. Some hung up or never responded. But some acknowledged that they had been affected by my choices. They had experienced doubt and regret. A few said they could forgive me.

I want to stress again how important it was for me to have these conversations in the presence of a trusted Christian. Because I still felt vulnerable to these memories, I needed backup to make sure that seeking forgiveness didn't lead to more sin. But as I acknowledged and faced my past, I began to see these men through God's eyes, and I could truly feel free from this interpersonal entanglement of lust, memory, and nostalgia. What's more, even for the men who couldn't acknowledge our activity as harmful, I knew they at least had to acknowledge that there was a different way of looking at it. I prayed our conversation might help them to seek the truth and mercy of Jesus, and then, in prayer, I released them to the Lord. I can gladly say that through the one-two punch of prayer and seeking forgiveness, my mind became free from the power of memories that were once my constant companions. Though far from perfect, I have a clarity of mind and heart regarding

---

[95] For more on becoming aware of the effects of our sin on others, see Comiskey, *Living Waters*, Chapter 6.

my sexual choices that I never thought possible. Entering into the battle both spiritually and relationally, with Jesus and other trustworthy disciples, ensures victories far beyond what we could ask or imagine.[96]

ON THE ROAD TO LIFE

Let's review the steps we've covered in this chapter. First, we've acknowledged that any freedom from sexually and relationally destructive patterns can only come through a complete surrender to Jesus, allowing Him to define how we give and receive love. We looked at the importance of complete honesty with God and with trusted Christians that dispels the power and shame of a dark, hidden life. And we opened ourselves, however unwillingly, to the concept of boundaries — both spiritual and practical — as essential for our protection.

I am most grateful for the men who walked with me in my early days of following Jesus, who always took me back to being a *doer* of the Word of God, not a hearer only.[97] After taking in a chapter with so many directives, could I invite you to examine how to put action to these concepts?

- *Have you fully surrendered your greatest area of temptation or struggle to Jesus's Lordship and authority? If not, how can you practically forsake everything as loss for the sake of knowing and following Jesus?*

- *Have you become honest with someone about your sin? Do you have secrets that need to be brought into the light of a godly relationship so they can lose their power over you? If so, who might you talk to this week?*

- *Have you set appropriate boundaries with technology? In your worst moment of your worst day, would you have easy access to defiling or pornographic material? If so, consider purchasing Covenant Eyes or a comparable source of internet boundaries and accountability.*

---

[96] Ephesians 3:20
[97] James 1:22

- *Have you released the power of Jesus to break the power of illicit relationships from your past? If not, stop and assert the resurrection power of Jesus over dead works of past sin. Ask Holy Spirit to release your mind, body, soul, spirit, and memory from the ravages of sin.*

- *Have you taken spiritual authority in prayer over demonic influences in your life?*

- *Is there anyone you have sinned against, with whom you need to seek forgiveness or reconciliation? If so, stop reading, "leave your gift on the altar,"[98] and go make things right with your Christian sister or brother.*

These concepts are extremely important as we acknowledge where we find ourselves today: grappling with the consequences of our sin and seeking to walk above what has entangled us. There is powerful healing to be found in each of these as they address the biggest problems we face before God: the battles of humility versus pride, and intimacy versus shame. I like to think of these steps as directives that get us back on the narrow road that leads to life. They aren't necessarily all of life itself. To become a people who move beyond sobriety into true transformation, we cannot neglect these values — they are the foundation to a full life in Jesus.

As we move along the narrow road, however, we find we need more — we aren't satisfied with patting ourselves on the back for staying sober. In this next chapter, we'll build on the essential foundations and explore how we gradually gain hearts that are both cleared of the grief of sin and full of the passionate love of Jesus poured out for everyone we encounter.

---

[98] Mathew 5:24

Chapter Eight

DEEPENING FOUNDATIONS

"Everything in human nature resists divine grace, because grace changes us and change is painful."

Flannery O'Connor

If we're honest, we've all had experiences with Christians who were not likely committing any "felonies" in the arena of their sexuality and relationships, yet who didn't exactly strike us as prototypes of passionate and full living. Indeed, the secular world has looked at much of the church's expression of sexual purity and deemed our lives as boring, lifeless, neutered. No wonder they see our stances for Biblical authenticity and hear only law and judgment. How do we become a people who experience extravagant joy in intimacy, the "life to the fullest" that Jesus came to earth to win for us?[99]

In my role as the Counseling Pastor at a church with a large demographic of college students, young adults, and young families, we've had many challenges that are typical to communities like ours. Many come to our church with a pure passion for missions, a desire to change the world for God, but with little sense of their personal identity and even less understanding of their historic vulnerabilities and wounds.

When I assumed my role a few years ago, our church was very strong in promoting God's heart for the nations, but we weren't as good at promoting God's heart for the holistic healing of the soul. Our

---

[99] John 10:10

church had a value for freedom but didn't talk about how Christians heal from deep-seated struggles such as shame, pornography addiction, same-sex attraction, or surviving abuse. Most of our members would look at a struggler and say, full of faith, "Jesus will set you free," but wouldn't have clear answers as to how that happens. We had a lot of faith and vision for Jesus's healing power but little practical help to offer a struggler.

It's been my great joy to see Jesus develop our church, to see our members grow not just numerically but also in the depth of their understanding of Jesus's healing and saving work, especially as it applies to our familiar areas of brokenness. We now know some things that work and some things that don't, and we have easy on-ramps for people to begin a process of healing, redemption, and transformation. For churches to live out the Great Commission in a generation where broken families are the norm, we *must* partner our good outreach with an equally good inreach, including an expansive vision for deep healing and restoration. Only then will we have missionaries and evangelists who know the deep, healing love of Jesus as well as they know evangelism skills.

Jesus uses the power of prayer to restore a sense of identity, hope and security to each of us. I have found that, regardless of what specific struggles Christians face, a few keys are fundamental to receiving and giving love in ways that foster a true joy in the face of life, a whole-hearted joy that's neither naive nor compromised. *This* is what the world is hungry for, and the rarest of finds in our day. Like Paul, I don't claim that I have laid hold of it,[100] but all my disqualifications aside, I'd like to explore some components of healing and transformation that help us live in a place of radical joy and transformation through the power of the Holy Spirit.

HOW LONG IS THIS GOING TO TAKE?

I love hearing stories of people who get zapped by God and change instantly. This happens physically all the time — a headache suddenly lifts, deaf ears are opened, a tumor disappears, and we rightfully rejoice at the extravagant power and kindness of God. I've heard a few stories of these kinds of instant changes happening with regard to a sexual

---

[100] Phil. 3:12

addiction or a struggle with intimacy, but often the process of healing and change seems painfully slow as it regards our most vulnerable and intimate areas.

Why is that? Is God's power shortened when it comes to our relational longings? Do we simply lack the faith or the keys to see long-standing proclivities instantly removed?

While I absolutely believe God is capable of anything and always wants to bring greater and deeper revelation to us, maybe God has something deeper in his heart than simply delivering us from our vulnerabilities.[101] I've had the privilege of witnessing the process of transformation for many people — it's always unique, it's always painful, and it's *always* been slower than the individual wants.

In the midst of the journey, though, I regularly see a subtle but seismic shift happen in the hearts of those on the road of life. At some point, they realize that God is more interested in loving them than in "fixing" their problems. Often, underneath their frustration of cyclical weakness lies a fear that their weakness makes them unworthy of love. They wonder if God is frowning on them because they struggle with the same old things that they struggled with six days, six weeks, six months, or six years ago.

This fear of being found unworthy of love is something more important to God than an instantaneous transportation from perversion to purity. Just like children, we are learning what the language of heaven sounds like, and what the love of heaven looks like. We fumble and fall many times as we learn to walk, and God wouldn't have it any other way, because He actually loves the learning.

Another reality I've found is that while many factors contribute to any kind of brokenness — physical, emotional, or spiritual — often in the realm of sexual and relational frustrations, current struggles stem from long-standing wounds. As we've seen, these wounds are often rooted in early childhood trauma or foundational relationships that went sour and set up a young, vulnerable heart to misunderstand love and intimacy.

As a result, healing necessitates the power of the Holy Spirit not only to empower a life of current freedom, but also to reveal Himself

---

[101] For a masterful work on process and hope, see John Pieper, *On Hope*.

as the God who *was*; to unveil the points in time where love became distorted and unravel each of those moments individually until a heart that had been a tangled mess becomes clear and free from all entanglements. In a radically broken world, for most of us the entanglements are many. But as we say "yes" to a lengthy education in our histories and in love, we marvel at God's loving patience and begin to understand that He not only wants to heal us, but He also wants us secure in His love in the midst of our ongoing inadequacies.

GETTING TO THE ROOT

Considering our historical deficits, I thought it would be helpful to describe a few areas of deeper healing common to the process of relational restoration. You can think of these as healing "pit-stops" on the road to wholeness. They're important to visit — the road of learning love is one we certainly don't want to short-circuit. Yet none of these is *home* — camp out too long on any of them and you'll find yourself lost in introspection, looking inside rather than towards the greater life of the Kingdom. If we can visit these areas with the help of a trusted counselor, prayer minister, pastor, or even a wise friend, we'll find our hearts significantly freer from clutter and obstacle, and more able to fully comprehend the love of God that surpasses all knowledge.[102]

A NOTE ON "CONVERSION THERAPY"

Particularly when relational and sexual struggles involve gender dysphoria or same-sex attraction, a concern often arises regarding "conversion therapy," so I thought it might be helpful to address that concern here.

We should all have a healthy concern about any sort of therapeutic or pastoral intervention that is coercive, abusive, or shame-inducing. The purpose of any counseling or pastoral help should include a *reduction* or *removal* of shame and guilt, along with an increase in faith, hope, and security. This is biblical: a godly sorrow produces repentance, while an ungodly shame produces death.[103] As Christians, we can and should stand against any person seeking the harm of a vulnerable individual who is asking for help.

---

[102] Ephesians 3:19
[103] 2 Corinthians 7:10

I have heard accounts of horrendous treatment of individuals who felt coerced into practices that a counselor allegedly suggested to reduce same-sex attractions. My heart broke as I heard one man describe having his mouth filled with marbles by a counselor who purported that this would decrease his same-sex attraction. This man felt abused and shamed, as if some deformity in his mouth was causing his sexual attractions. We should weep at the thought of vulnerable individuals being made to feel defective in this way.

Unfortunately, the term "conversion therapy" was coined for a different purpose. Rather than describing clear theory or tactics, "conversion therapy" is a phrase that was specifically created to include any mindset or belief system that affirms that a person can overcome unwanted same-sex attraction or gender dysphoria. I have been unable to find a therapist who claims to offer "conversion therapy" because it simply doesn't exist as a therapeutic model; it exists only as an accusation regarding a worldview.

Other therapeutic models, such as cognitive behavioral therapy or psychodynamics, describe processes that therapists can be trained in and that can be evaluated for effectiveness. By "conversion therapy," critics aren't discussing a specific therapeutic process, but are discussing a person's ability to choose and achieve gender security and healthy heterosexual relationships. As Christians, we can and should stand for any person seeking to assist others who voluntarily wish to come into alignment with their birth gender and their ingrained, bodily call to healthy same-gender friendships and heterosexual relationships.

As we journey with individuals whom we love and care for as they seek greater maturity and holiness, we should always celebrate the brave steps forward. We should affirm that the choice of what help to receive, when to receive it, and from whom is their decision alone. We want to hold high the standard of Jesus's call to righteousness while also holding high the dignity of an individual's choice to ask for help when and how they need it as they seek Jesus's righteousness.

That disclaimer is true here as well. Feel no pressure to press into any of these areas of healing. Hear only an invitation to press into the areas that Holy Spirit highlights as helpful for your breakthrough and growth in godly love and relationships.

RESTORATION OF RESPONSE

Because nurture and trust are the first things we're supposed to learn in life, God is passionate about restoring in each of us a hearty acceptance of our needs and a trusting sense of His loving acceptance and provision for our needs in the way that a mother nurtures a treasured infant. It should come as no surprise to us that this restoration happens primarily in the place of prayer, through the brooding presence of the Holy Spirit.[104]

So often, our prayer lives are anxious, driven, or overly linear. We have our list of people we pray for or situations in the world over which to proclaim truths. Perhaps in the midst of our prayerful activity we could all benefit from slowing down and focusing on the quiet presence of God as He invisibly imparts His love into our hearts.

This is difficult for our busy culture and even more difficult for those with addictive tendencies. We want a quick fix, not a God who simply *is*.[105] Yet, God, whose name is I AM, is waiting for us with all the peace and love we really need. Experiencing healing from the constant companions of anxiety and inner noise produces more fruit than we could imagine — our desire for love becomes contained as we know it will get met. Our needs become peaceful invitations into intimacy rather than exaggerated demands we place on others. Our problems become gateways into intimacy rather than trap doors into isolation and medication. Our desire for comfort results in prayer to El Shaddai (literally "The Breasted One") rather than binges into pornographic images of women.

PRACTICING GOD'S HEALING PRESENCE

To begin practicing this kind of quiet meditation on the presence of God, place your hands over the center of yourself (for most people this is in the chest or abdomen) and invite the Holy Spirit to come. Don't worry about complicated prayers to pray. Simply enjoy and focus on the reality of the Healing Presence surrounding and filling you with a love that doesn't leak out but rather heals the cracks in your heart. If you have a trusted caregiver (Christian counselor, mentor) who can pray

---

[104] For more on practicing the presence of God, see Leanne Payne, *The Healing Presence*, p. 25-34
[105] Exodus 3:14

with you, have them place their hands over your hands as a physical sign of the God who is *with you*, and stay there for a good chunk of time while you soak in the enjoyment of simply being loved with no strings attached. If you're alone, allow yourself to breathe deeply in and out and feel the hidden, yet sufficient provision God has for you. Do this not one time but regularly to find solace and peace through healthy intimacy with God.

UNITING WITH OUR FATHER

While many people can look at their mothers and honestly say, "She did the best she could," we live in an age where fathers are often nowhere to be found. Sometimes a father has left the family through divorce, choosing to brush off the "constraints" of family life to exercise his "freedom." Other times a father has left through addiction, be it to pornography or alcohol or work. When these things happen, at any level, a mark is made on a child's view of masculinity.[106]

When dads abandon their families through unfaithfulness, divorce, or addiction, true faithfulness and provision are distorted in the minds and hearts of children. Many times, children are left wondering if the divorce was *their* fault. This can set an individual up for adult relationships where the greatest fear is being found unworthy of true faithfulness and generosity.

Sometimes a wounding relationship with a father can be focused more on what Dad didn't do rather than what he *did* do. My dad was always physically present in the home and was faithful to my family in countless ways. Due to his own childhood molestation and trauma, my dad was emotionally distant. He hugged me, but he hugged me in a way that failed to impart a powerful sense of love and identity. He'd ask about my school and hobbies, but I never felt known by him. Sadly, this kind of emotional neglect is quite common and results in a child lurching into the world with a weakened sense of worth or competence.

For me, a lack of this kind of intimate relationship was part of what resulted in my experiencing same-sex attraction in my teenage years. I absolutely do not blame my dad for my same-sex attraction. What I see is that underneath my same-sex attraction was a desire to feel intimately

---

[106] See Leanne Payne, *Crisis in Masculinity*.

known and connected to a man who knew more than me, who could tell me who I was. I share that need with every other man on earth. For many men, that need is met through healthy father-son relationships, friendships, or mentorships, and never becomes sexualized.

So how do we encounter the healing of Jesus in a way that frees us to know the Father? First, I believe we must recognize and name the weakness we feel for what it really is. We must mourn what we needed and never got from our earthly fathers, rather than believing an achievement or human relationship can provide the ultimate sense of security, affection, or recognition for which we long.[107]

Secondly, we must forgive our fathers, fully and completely. Unforgiveness toward parents inevitably means repeating their mistakes, but a forgiving heart can joyfully receive the provision of God through parents as well as the greater Body of Christ.

As we search the Scriptures and begin to perceive the adoption God offers us, we learn to pray boldly the way Jesus teaches us to pray. We plainly ask for our "daily bread" — unashamedly make known what we need physically, spiritually, emotionally, relationally — and then we sit back as God answers us through His Holy Spirit and through the community of faith He set in place. Our souls lose their orphaned spirit that says we must make a way for ourselves, and a quiet sets in as we come to know the God that "will fight for you, you need only to be silent."[108]

A BLESSED INHERITANCE

In her seminal book *Crisis in Masculinity*, Leanne Payne states that a man who is not at peace with his father is not at peace with his masculinity. That convicted me when I looked at my history of a fractured sense of masculinity that paired with a chronic sense of disappointment in the level of closeness I achieved with my dad. A radical breakthrough for me came in prayer when I began to speak forgiveness over my father for what I perceived he didn't give me. I forgave him for abandoning me through his suicide. I forgave him for failing to connect with me in the way I wanted and needed.

After I repented for my unforgiving heart, I asked Jesus to show

---

[107] Comiskey, *Living Waters*, page 65
[108] Exodus 14:14

me what He gave to me specifically through my father. I received those things as a gift from my Heavenly Father. I thanked God that my dad went to work every day and gave the money he earned to provide for me and my siblings, and I received that inheritance of faithfulness and provision. I thanked God that my dad served my family by doing chores regularly, and I asked for more of that spirit of service.

As I prayed this way, I could feel a creative miracle happening in my masculinity. No longer was I choosing to believe I was incomplete, a victim of abandonment, a man working with less relational muscle because I lacked intimacy in my childhood. I felt genuine gratefulness for who my dad was and genuine joy at who God created me to be. I was able to release my dad from his sins because I stood on the truth that God had "delivered me from the empty way of life handed down by my forefathers."[109] Through His death, Jesus severed any brokenness in my heritage, and He multiplied and purified all the good aspects of my lineage through the power of the resurrection. This peace with my dad gave me greater confidence in my relationships and greater empowerment in my sense of identity.

Of course, this healing must be worked out in human relationships as well. God continually uses men and women in the church to remind us of our conflictual relationships with parents and siblings so that we might press through for more healing. For me, good Christian men have mentored me into maturity, and at some point in these relationships, there comes a time when the man reminds me of one of my parents and I want to run away.

Thankfully, in the mercy of God, Holy Spirit shows me the underlying issue and uses difficult seasons in relationships to point me to greater forgiveness, greater acceptance, and greater relational wholeness and integrity. I begin to love older and younger men and women in the Body simply because they're worthy of love, imperfect, yet beautiful. I stop expecting them to become the lost father or mother of my youth. They don't have to give me ultimate direction, affirmation, or purpose, because God is already meeting that need beautifully. I can receive other people with a joyful heart and without the perverted expectations that ruin intimacy.

---

[109] 1 Peter 1:18

I see this play out in "discipleship" relationships all the time. The discipler starts out in the disciple's eyes as all-knowing, arrived, all-wise. The disciple is willing to do whatever his discipler says. Until the mentor isn't available to respond to a phone call or text. Until the mentor responds judgmentally or breaks trust. At that point, he goes from being a demigod to being the enemy — untrustworthy, another example of human disappointment. Might we see in these frustrating moments an opportunity to step into a more mature and holistic way of viewing one another as co-inheritors of mercy and favor we don't deserve? Might Jesus be healing our wounds through the very aspects of relationship that are most frustrating to us? I believe that, for those who press through such frustrations and process them with the Holy Spirit and other wise counselors, there's a gift of security and wholeness awaiting to us.

DEVELOPING ENDURANCE

Why do some people seem to thrive in Jesus for a span of time, then suddenly fade into the shadows of compromise, hiddenness, and disillusionment? This question has brought about some of my greatest pain, both as a friend and as a pastor. It's heartbreaking to see people begin the process of healing, only to lose their momentum. At best, this can look like a cyclical pattern of rebellion, repentance, and restoration, only to be repeated with the next stressor. At worst, this has led to beloved leaders using their new-found empowerment to lead others into humanistic philosophy, offense toward church leadership, and moral compromise.

As church leaders, we shouldn't be surprised, introspective, or intimidated by the schemes of the enemy to divide our churches and church members. Jesus promised this dynamic would come into play in Mark 4 in the parable of the sower of the seed. He promised that some would fail to receive truth because of demonic oppression, some would thrive until things got difficult, some would begin to grow until they desired something more than the simplicity of the gospel, and some would endure, mature, and bear fruit.

I have found that as a leader, I must train people to identify when they may come into each of these seasons.[110] As we walk with people into freedom and wholeness, we also must set them up for the expectation of a life lived in human weakness, dependent on the strength of an Almighty Savior. That way, when we experience seasons of disappointment, weakness and difficulty, we are less prone to redefine our theology or reinterpret truth, and we are better able to laugh at our present difficulties and get back on the road to life.

While these seasons of refining happen individually, they also happen in the life of the church. As our churches face the important topics of gender, sexuality, and paths of healing in these areas, it will mean a testing for our church members. The sad truth is many don't want us to get clear on morality and sexuality; many prefer these issues be left alone entirely or left for each confused and wounded church member to navigate alone however they "feel led."

When I've experienced that kick-back, or navigated the grief of someone I love choosing a life in the shadows over life with Jesus in the light, my tendency is to be obsessive, introspective, and focus on what I should have done differently to make everyone like me and like Jesus. This is when I must remind myself that loving another is truly committing them into the hands of Jesus, rather than seeking to control, manipulate, and tend to my reputation and image.

What I can't do in these situations is alter my values and beliefs for the sake of popularity and relationship. If I'm not authentic to Jesus first and foremost, and authentic to His call on my life inside my friendships and relationships, then I'm not a safe and truth-telling friend. What I can do is extend my concern and commitment and point my friends toward Jesus. If they choose this, they can know they have an open door to me. If they choose to pursue lust instead, there's nothing I can do to stop them, and there's nothing I can do to keep the shame of sin from attaching to them. I must release them to Jesus and rededicate myself to Him before and above any human relationship.

Whether we find ourselves discouraged by the difficulty of our own battles, or disappointed by the response of others, we must learn to discern when the enemy is coming to steal, kill, and destroy our lives. We must ask for and exercise the classic Christian virtues of fortitude (a strength of spirit that overcomes obstacles) and magnanimity (a commitment to aspire to greatness in the face of persistent struggles and

---

[110] Stephen Black, *Freedom Realized*, "The Burden of Those Who Do Not Finish the Race"

weaknesses)[111] as we receive the life of the Spirit who comes that we might have life, and life abundant.[112]

Freedom from life-dominating sin is possible. It should the norm for those in Jesus. Oppression and compromise should be abnormal for a follower of Jesus. Through resolving the wounds of the heart, receiving and offering forgiveness, and engaging in spiritual battle, our minds can truly be transformed into a new way of thinking.[113]

---

[111] Josef Pieper, *On Hope*, p. 27-28
[112] John 10:10
[113] Romans 12:1-2

Chapter Nine

RELATIONSHIPS THAT HEAL

"As I have loved you, so also you must love one another."
John 13:34

"Perhaps all our loves are merely hints and symbols."
Evelyn Waugh, Brideshead Revisited

As we discover the freedom Jesus gives us, we naturally (or, rather, supernaturally) desire to give pure love away. Love must always have an object, and once we've surrendered to Jesus, we begin to see His invitations to engage with people who need and deserve love. Once we discover the desire to "love from a pure heart and a clean conscience,"[114] the question surfaces of just what *is* healthy love? In our world, we have numerous examples of lustful, possessive, romanticized love, and far less vision for a love that seeks another's interest above its own.[115]

When I first began to walk with Jesus, I wanted all my healing to happen alone with God. Relationships were where I had experienced the most pain and hurt. For me, going to a "guy's night" was more intimidating than trying a new worship experience, prayer exercise, or Bible study. In truth, even today relationships can be tricky ground for me. Pressing into conflict where necessary, believing the best about my friends or spouse, and serving others in ways that are costly all test what

---

[114] 1 Timothy 1:5
[115] Philippians 2:4

I say I believe in and cause me to actually grow into the image of Jesus.

So as we enter the realm of relationships, we run many risks of "getting it wrong" — finding ourselves loving selfishly or hurting others when our true heart longs to heal. But risk we must! Healing can never occur in a vacuum, and maturity requires that we step out into the glorious and messy world of life-on-life intimacy, be it in friendship, dating, or marriage. Just as Jesus endured suffering for the joy of gaining a Bride and the family of the church, so must we endure the difficult work of gaining sobriety and healing, not as an end in itself, but rather for the purpose of being able to give ourselves to the church and its members wholeheartedly, healthily, and joyfully.

HEALTHY SAME-SEX FRIENDSHIPS

Just as babies must learn to crawl before they learn to walk, so must we all learn first to walk with God and forsake our sin, then to procure godly same-sex friendships, and after that to learn how to honor and bless the opposite gender.[116] In good same-sex friendships, we learn the essential skills of working out conflicts and disappointments, and managing our expectations and affections appropriately.

Beginning to step out into healthy friendships can be more difficult than it seems. On one side, we're susceptible to "faking it." We wear masks. We pretend to be more confident, more stereotypical, more victorious than we actually feel in an attempt to protect ourselves from familiar rejection. On the other hand, we battle needing too much from our friends. I have often gone through the cycle of feeling the pull to isolate, choosing to reach out and expose my real needs and fears, then feeling disappointed at the response, or lack of response, I get in return.

These are the points where my faith gets tested. Will I live in faith that God can meet my needs and provide good and imperfect friends to reciprocate my good and imperfect offering? I've found a few themes that have helped me in moving from isolation and narcissism into healthy friendships with men.

FRIENDSHIPS TAKE TIME

In our day and age where virtually everything is instant, friendships

---

[116] Nicolosi, *Shame and Attachment Loss*, p. 303-316; Comiskey, *Living Waters*, Chapter 14.

are a great reality check that "good things take time." When I lived in the musical theatre community, my norm was instant intimacy — within the course of a 2-week rehearsal period, I'd have a new "best friend" who knew everything about me and spent every waking moment with me. The next show or school semester often involved a transition into a new enmeshment. My friends typically held the same interests as I did, used the same language, and made the same jokes.

Friendships in the kingdom of God are different. Here, our common bond is Jesus, and because He serves as our ultimate source of love, we are able to endure the length of time required to develop lasting bonds while maintaining our individual calling and identity.[117]

Time allows us to appreciate a same-sex friend's unique gender expression. When I began to hang out with healthy Christian guys, it was hard for me to know what to talk about if I wasn't talking about musical theatre or film. My initial tendencies were either to lose myself in pretending to be just like someone else, in an attempt to ward off rejection, or require that my friends care about my exact passions in order to be deemed safe.

At first, hanging out around a campfire with other guys felt boring and uncomfortable, but it gave me time to hear what interested them — to hear where they'd come from, how they looked at life and approached challenges, and what made them come alive. I began to hold my interests and passions a little more loosely, relishing times when I could talk about my love for music and literature but accepting those interests as one expression of masculinity rather than something at odds with another guy's masculinity.

This can be a big challenge. A lure of the gay community is that it separates "us" (men who talk like me, think like me, act like me, have similar interests as me) from "them" (men who live more comfortably with traditional masculinity). Without embracing the time it takes for these false dividing walls to be torn down, we stay in camps that prevent growth and maturity. In the same way, overcoming pornography or sexual addiction must also involve forsaking "surface" friendship in favor of deep vulnerability, honesty, and interdependency with friends who challenge and point us to Jesus's best for our lives.

---

[117] Dietrich Bonhoeffer's *Life Together* speaks profoundly on Christ-centered friendship.

We must recognize and forsake isolation and dividing walls. The addict got addicted in secrecy and isolation; the Christ-follower becomes sober through radical honesty and the give and take of intimacy with friends. If I were to relate to male friends as a "gay" man, it would give me permission to continue to view myself as half-accepted. I might be "accepted," but accepted as someone inherently different from another man. Instead, removing labels allows me to relate to other men as an equally legitimate man, called to the same masculinity of initiation and courage, while simply seeing hobbies, interests, and specific struggles as the side-notes that they are. Instead of running toward comfort when friendships aren't immediately easy, perseverance allows intimacy, mutual respect, and appreciation to develop into a relationship that both secures and challenges both parties.

OVERCOMING EMOTIONAL DEPENDENCY

Once trust and comfort are built into a friendship, we must simultaneously tend to the friendship while releasing the friend to their own unique calling. Friendships that give both support and space allow both friends to flourish, while friendships that possess and close in toward exclusivity can easily become destructive and dependent. Emotional dependency on a friend occurs when "the ongoing presence and nurturing of another is believed to be necessary for personal security."[118]

I have a good friend who has struggled with the pull of emotional dependency. A daughter of an alcoholic, she never felt fully prioritized and valued in her formative years; instead, those years were marked by significant neglect and the anxiety of her parents' divorce. As an adult, she experienced an acute longing for a "special friend" — someone who would call her first, who would make herself available when she's in need, someone who could give her the preference she never experienced growing up.

When good friends seemed too busy or involved with other friends, her heart became both triggered and tested. All the familiar messages would begin to replay in her mind — "I love her more than she loves me," "No one really cares," "I'm too much for people." In her immaturity, she would buy into these messages and put her frustrations and

---

[118] Lori Rentzel, *Emotional Dependency*, p. 7.

expectations onto her developing friendships, which would distance her friends and repeat the cycle of rejection and neglect. However, as she's grown and matured, this incredible woman has learned to bring her vulnerabilities to Jesus. With Him, she is reminded of a Friend who went through death itself to secure her in love, and that love makes her able to spread her relational needs to several friends and stand in faith and gratefulness for the good and imperfect friends that offer her good and imperfect love. Her friends have become signs and symbols of a love that never fails, rather than all-or-nothing sources of worth.

OVERCOMING ISOLATION

While some overattach to a special friend, others struggle to attach at all. Healthy friendship requires reaching outside of self, even and especially when it feels more desirable to isolate. After growing up in a home environment where I was often subject to bullying, I have regularly had to confront a desire to begin detaching from friendship in order to take care of my problems on my own. When I feel vulnerable and in need, I also feel the most walled off.

In light of this, some of my most healing memories in friendship have occurred when I faced my needs and weaknesses with one or two trusted friends. I remember a season when I was particularly seeking to overcome a cyclical struggle with masturbation. While I knew that God loved me even when I messed up, I also knew I didn't want to be mastered by anything and that my body wasn't designed to complete itself sexually — I wanted to feel the ache for intimate relationship as a single man without escaping into a private fantasy world of self-pleasure. God challenged me to reach out to one or two friends every time I had even a *thought* about masturbating.

I didn't like this challenge at all. Every time I had such a thought, my next thought inevitably was a temptation just to pray and make it through the day sober on my own with Jesus. After all, I had random thoughts about masturbating *a lot*. That would overwhelm anyone, right?

The thing is, the challenge worked. Every time I would reach out in my earliest and easiest temptations, someone would respond over the course of the next few days with a prayer or a follow-up about my sobriety. Often, someone would respond almost immediately. I began to understand that I was going to be seen by my friends, not just in my public face, but in my private moments of doubt and struggle as well, and that knowledge motivated me to live privately in alignment with the values I publicly professed.

One friend God had challenged me to reach out to in this season was a bit of a challenge for me. His personality was intense, and he took truth very seriously. You might even call him rigid — I sure did. Once when I texted this friend to check off my box of obedience (I'm sure something deep like "temped to masturbate"), he immediately texted and said, "Thanks for telling me. DON'T! I'm coming over now," and I wanted to disappear. I was simply informing him of my struggle — I didn't want to see or talk to him. But he came right on over and invaded my privacy and began talking with me about life. Pretty soon, we had one of our best conversations about the loneliness we were both facing as single men. I think we went swimming. And I didn't have another thought about fantasizing. My need to be seen and known was being met by a simple afternoon with a trustworthy friend.

Particularly for anyone overcoming sexually-addictive tendencies, developing deep attachments with same-gendered friends is essential. It delivers us from the facade of a public "good boy" and a private rebel who takes care of himself. More importantly, it builds trust that others can truly offer love that is fulfilling, an antidote to the visceral, sickening thrill of fantasy and orgasm.

HEALTHY HETEROSEXUALITY

Whatever our past brokenness and present vulnerabilities may be, all of us who follow Jesus have been called to model Jesus's dignifying love toward the opposite gender. I believe that learning to love the opposite gender well is at the basis of our most important and most challenging life-long lessons of discipleship. Indeed, generations to come will be affected by who men will be for women and what women will be for men. Each of us has unique challenges stemming from our unique pasts but facing these challenges and seeking to offer pure love roots us squarely in dependence on Holy Spirit and offers us the joy of experiencing His supernatural love.

For me, after years of constant dating in the gay community before giving my life to Jesus, I spent several painful years single and refusing to entertain even a notion of heterosexual dating. I didn't want to be fake and force a relationship that held no attraction to me, and I questioned whether a woman would ever appeal to me romantically.

In truth, these years were essential. They allowed me to learn about being a man in relation to God and how to be a friend to other men. In friendship with a handful of trustworthy guys who were also pursuing Jesus, I learned how to keep my desire for intimacy clear from romantically fantasizing about my friends, and I learned how to press in rather than run away when I didn't feel safe or accepted.

As the years passed, I relived the process most boys experience in puberty. I began to see that I *did* have healthy friendships with several men, I wasn't unhealthily isolating, yet I was still lonely. Hanging out with more traditionally masculine guys wasn't scary or exotic to me anymore; in fact, it became kind of boring. I began to notice the women around me, not as potential buddies, but as these beautiful expressions of compassion, revelation, and joy. Indeed, achieving healthy and fulfilling same-sex friendships will inevitably lead to an exposure of just what these friendships are *not*, which is romantic.

For someone with a more "traditional" background of porn addiction, the road to sanctification may look less like awakening desire and more like reigning in lustful passion in order to recognize a member of the opposite sex for his/her *dignity*, not just his/her sex appeal. Then, after learning to be sober and becoming a truth-telling friend, a man or woman may begin to experience Holy Spirit challenging him/her to take a risk in engaging in a godly romantic relationship where the pace of growing intimacy comes not from lust-riddled hormones, but from prayerful dependence on God and godly counselors.

I want to re-emphasize the progression here. I've met with many young men who jump from dating relationship to dating relationship (or at least crush to crush) out of fantasy. Isolated and addicted, they see women as a distraction from a mundane life. I've also had to counsel same-sex strugglers against pursuing heterosexuality as an attempt to "fix" oneself before pursuing personal wholeness and healthy same-sex friendships. Only out of the overflow of a secure identity and fulfilling friendships can a man truly offer himself to a woman for her good and dignity. For us to truly step into the gift of our own gender, we have to learn to relate honorably to the opposite gender.[119]

While same-sex friendships can be a bit of a challenge, particularly for those with a background of rejection, dating relationships potentially leading to marriage are downright intimidating. What's worse, often young adults are given no more guidance than "Don't have sex," as if this gives a good plan to achieving relationships that are mutually enjoyable and dignifying. So what can help us achieve healthy heterosexual relationships?

HONOR

Because of the nature of my ministry, books about sexuality and dating are often recommended to me. One dynamic that bothers me as a pastor is the lack of good equipping literature that details how to date well. Much more often, I see literature devoted to "courtship" or models of romance that seem prudish and distrustful that dating relationships can look like the Kingdom of God. This lack of biblical equipping opens a big door for young adults in the church to look to popular media and secular culture to find how a real-life romance can work in the 21st century. I regularly talk with young people in various stages of dating relationships and ask myself how to father young men in my church to lead and pursue women with honor, but without some of the more conventional religious weirdness.

Remember that love compels us to "look not only to our own interest, but also to the interest of others." One of the best ways we can become an extension of Jesus's love to the opposite gender is to think first about what would most bless and honor her, rather than emphasizing what makes me look cool or feel good.

One of the reasons that personal sobriety is such an important prerequisite for healthy dating is that healthy dating relationships require a growing level of self-mastery. We must exercise our power to choose what is best for the other when it conflicts with what feels good.

Before I dated Jordyn, I had one other significant heterosexual dating experience, where I largely failed at advocating for her good above my own emotions and feelings. The relationship wasn't sinful,

---

[119] John Paul II, *TOB*, 43:7

but it was an emotional roller-coaster, a tough yet necessary mirror to show me my immaturities and difficulties at translating my healthy devotional life in God into becoming a trustworthy source of love and dignity for a woman. Although I was getting distance from homosexuality and addiction, I still hadn't become a safe leader for a woman's heart.

When I began dating Jordyn a few years later, I was a bit more mature and aware of how my actions affected her. I certainly didn't do everything great in my dating relationship with Jordyn, but I did begin communicating early and often about boundaries and expectations in our dating relationship, and I tried my best to live up to my words. Whether our relationship lasted for 2 dates, 20 dates, or a lifetime, I wanted us both to feel no regret, and I committed myself to her feeling valued, honored, and considered throughout our relationship.

Honoring Jordyn didn't just mean expressing my thoughts on boundaries and the pace of the relationship, it meant truly opening myself to hear from her. Sometimes she would need to express how my boundaries affected her and made her feel, and honoring her meant that I listened to her perspective with an openness to change. Getting over my pride meant that I had to grow in understanding how my actions affected a woman and how I might better express my affection for her through better words and actions. What a gift!

JESUS-CENTEREDNESS

Although Jordyn and I certainly weren't praying together on every date, an element that allowed us to experience joy and peace in our dating relationship was that we both understood that we went to Jesus to get our needs met first and foremost. Now some years into our marriage, this still is a marker of when we are doing well and when we aren't. When it feels like Jordyn constantly irritates me, chances are I'm looking to her to meet needs in me that she doesn't need to fill. Only when my connection with Jesus and my connections with friends are strong can I give myself to Jordyn's best interest rather than looking to her to make sure I'm safe and secure.

As we got serious in our dating relationship, I remember a conversation in which Jordyn told me some of what God was doing in her through our dating relationship. She expressed that, after her background of idolizing a romantic partner, she was realizing that "I'm never going to find a man that I love more than Jesus." As she spoke those words to me, desire washed over me for this woman who knew the Love above all Loves and was looking to me not to be the definition of love in her life, but simply an example of Christ's love for her. I fell more deeply in love with her in that moment.

All of us, in our immaturity, look at people of the opposite sex and begin to evaluate them based on an ideal in our minds. But as we begin to see that tendency as an expression of lust in our hearts, we can begin to appreciate members of the opposite sex, not to be evaluated against pros and cons, but as an expression of love from our Ultimate Love who is showing us the beauty and power of the opposite gender.

COMPLEMENTARITY

Honoring a dating partner or a spouse, while keeping Jesus central to our worship, also involves seeing the opposite gender's differences as an expression of glory, not liability. As we saw from the very beginning of the Creation accounts, men and women are made of different material and are given different callings and unique weaknesses. To the degree that we agree with Satan's view of the opposite gender, we will feel conflicted and frustrated in dating relationships or marriage. To the degree that we can value these differences and treasure them, we experience the joy that Jesus feels over His creation.

One of the things Jordyn and I did in our dating relationship was to ask a mentor to walk with us as we began dating seriously. We knew we'd come from difficult backgrounds in the realm of romance, so we were able to accept that we needed some help if we were going to move forward healthily with one another. Our mentor's name was John, and he quickly suggested an exercise for us. He asked us to make a list of the other person's positives — the things we saw in one another that made us come alive. Deep or shallow, spiritual or physical, we were learning to partner with Jesus to see the other through His eyes.

A few things happened in that exercise that changed me forever. One was that I could see and understand Jordyn's unique femininity in a new way. The things I saw in Jordyn that made me connect to Jesus's passion for her were often the very things that made me aware of just how different we were and just how differently we saw the world.

Whereas I was naturally driven, disciplined, and efficient, Jordyn loved children, saw the big picture, and lived in overcoming joy. Seeing just how differently she saw the world could lead to our biggest conflicts, but when I turned that around and prayed into those qualities, I could see what glorious strengths they were. This was such a different relationship than anything I had experienced in homosexuality — so full of the mystery of our differences and the calling to embrace these inherent differences rather than to conform into a replica of the other.

The other powerful component came when our mentor had us read our "positive list" to each other. When Jordyn read her positive list to me, I caught a glimpse of myself through her unique eyes and her process with Jesus. I heard her speak to the strength and resolve she saw in me, when I often saw myself as indecisive and weak. Indeed, experiencing this woman's view of my essence called me into the potential of my masculinity in a way that not even a great male friend could. I now saw my emerging masculine qualities not just as a goal for myself, but also as a gift that this woman needed and wanted. I truly began to learn who I was as a man as I gave myself to Jordyn.

FEARS, WALLS, AND DISAPPOINTMENTS

Just as in friendship, dating is sure to expose our fears of being abandoned, controlled, manipulated or neglected, and it's also sure to expose our broken reactions and responses to those fears and judgments.[120] We need good friends who will encourage us, comfort us, and call us up when heterosexual relationships seem like too much work to be worth it. We also need the good perspective of the opposite gender to challenge us to grow in godly character.

Though difficult to hear in the moment, some of Jordyn's responses when she experienced my walls and fears was essential to my growth into mature manhood. Because I had a gift and calling to lead in the relationship, and she to respond, my leadership would often reveal fears that she needed to bring to Jesus, and her responses revealed blind spots to me. Because I had experienced several times the damage of moving too fast in a dating relationship, my tendency toward Jordyn was to move our relationship at a snail's pace. When she'd ask me about

---

[120] Comiskey, *Living Waters*, Chapter 16

why my emotional, relational, and physical boundaries were staying the same month after month, I'd respond with my perspective of where we were at as a couple and what was appropriate. One time she gently, but firmly expressed that all of my "reasons" for caution in the relationship sounded like fear of commitment and that she needed me to figure out what I wanted because she wasn't interested being in an eternal dating relationship without clear direction.

It bugged me and it was true. I needed to hear it. I needed the relationship to grow me up. I needed her loving response to call me out of thinking, behaving, and speaking like a child — to become a man and put away childish things like self-protection and extreme caution.[121]

PHYSICAL INTIMACY

As Jordyn and I came into maturity, we became able to express our love in appropriate levels of physical intimacy. As I became mature enough to commit to her, I became trustworthy to exhibit this love through physical contact that became increasingly romantic as we moved through dating and engagement.

Since our wedding, Jordyn and I have found that healthy sexuality involves the whole person, not just our genital body parts. When I dedicate myself to serving and securing Jordyn, she opens herself to my love and becomes a source of wonderful affection and intimacy in return. The joy of our sex life is always interconnected with the success of our communication and emotional openness. When this holistic intimacy is in place, we can feel God smiling on our union of body, soul and spirit, and it transforms sex into an earthy and hearty act of worship.

TOWARDS COMMITMENT

While singleness, dating, and marriage are three wildly different realities, the core truth is that relationships are designed to call us up into a greater realization of the life of God in us. Friendships grow us out of isolation into interdependence, romance grows us out of pride and into collaboration, and marriage calls us out of independence into humility and patient perseverance. The same lessons that we learn in friendship and in dating continue to mature and deepen in us as we commit to the life-long road of intimacy in marriage.

---

[121] Comiskey, *Living Waters*, p. 348-349

As Jordyn and I moved out of dating and into marriage, we began to see the natural progression of intimacy. We realized our bond wasn't to serve the purpose of simple life-long mutual enjoyment, but to become a source of new life that we could only foster, support, and sustain together. While worldly love looks to self-pleasure, Kingdom love is always looking to where it can give itself away.

Because of this reality, I believe that marriages thrive when they are oriented around something bigger than personal growth and mutual satisfaction. When they are poured out into the fostering of young and vulnerable life, when they are given to the Kingdom purposes of healing the sick, remembering the poor, or providing a home for the lonely, marriages move out of being merely "happy" and into being signs pointing to heaven.

This requires more than just relational skills. It requires supernatural commitment, humility, and patience. But I know emphatically that the best expressions of love I have seen as a Christian have come from couples whose love for one another overflowed into welcoming me into their home — speaking life, encouragement and belief in me when I couldn't see those things for myself.

Whatever our season of life, our calling and our joy is to give ourselves away for Jesus, for His church, and for a world that desperately needs mothers and fathers to nurture and protect the most vulnerable. While our personal wholeness is necessary to bear fruit, only perseverance and faithfulness in relationship can bring forth this fruit. Our devotional and prayer life prepare us for the real world of friendships, dating, marriage, and ultimately parenting — pouring our lives out for the sake of those who need the good Jesus can offer through our willing and maturing "yes."

EPILOGUE

On April 6, 2013, one month shy of seven years after my "rock-bottom" experience in New York, I woke up to butterflies in my stomach. My best friend had stayed the night and picked up breakfast. As I met him in my kitchen that morning, reality slowly began to sink in: *I'm getting married today.* It felt so surreal, and as the morning unfolded, many of the men in my biological family came over and joined the men who had become my spiritual family over many years. This was a gathering of men who had believed that God had more for me when I couldn't believe that for myself, who had reminded me who I was when I felt lost and confused, who had chosen to welcome me into the fold and modeled humbly seeking God's very best for their lives without settling for moral compromise. They had seen me doing well and they had seen me cry, and they had stuck with me.

As we prepared for the ceremony, these brothers surrounded me and prayed over me. I don't remember any of their prayers, but I strongly remember the sense of belonging and celebration I felt. To stand in a room full of men who had shown me what love and friendship could be without becoming compromised or sexualized was humbling in itself, let alone in light of why we were gathered.

I arrived at our wedding venue to find many family and friends already there — a cloud of witnesses to Jesus's faithfulness in my and Jordyn's lives. Together, this group had seen us grow up, live in deep sin, endure broken relationships, reckon with salvation, and ultimately begin the life-long process of learning the way of Jesus's redemption and life.

As our wedding proceeded joyfully, I saw Jordyn, escorted by her father, walking down the aisle of this outdoor amphitheater. When we caught sight of each other, Jordyn just beamed and said "Hi!" and, from that moment through most of the rest of the ceremony, I giggled and laughed like a schoolboy. Joy simply overtook me.

It wasn't that I felt flippantly about the challenges of marriage and love. It wasn't the giddiness of denial or infatuation. The joy I felt was a kind of shock and awe. I kept thinking to myself, "Who'd have thought this would be my story?" For most of the 30 years of my life up to that point, heterosexual marriage with Jesus at the center felt simply outside the realm of possibilities for me. "Naked and unashamed" felt left behind in Eden. But as Jordyn walked down the aisle, I could feel Jesus giving me a little taste of what the wedding feast in the book of Revelation must be like: a sense of smallness and joyful gratitude as we, surrounded by the great cloud of witnesses to Jesus's faithfulness, get to experience a kind of intimacy that we don't deserve and never thought possible for ourselves. As Paul said to the Corinthians, "Now we see through a mirror dimly, but then we shall see face to face" (1 Corinthians 13:12).

I never knew it was possible to commit and covenant a life of intimacy that included as central the joy and celebration of God Himself, but now I know that this is God's desire for all of us. This is our very birthright as the children of God — a birthright to know holy love that is worth fight and sacrifice.

Married or single, I believe Jesus is making a people for Himself to serve as an answer and antidote to the offerings of cheap and compromised intimacy that proliferate our society. He's not intimated by the darkness because He knows how to make His people shine with "love that surpasses knowledge."[122]

By no means have Jordyn and I arrived. Our wedding day began a new chapter in our lives that has included greater challenges than we could have ever foreseen. Together we have endured the life-threatening illness of our oldest son, different beliefs about God's calling for our family, painful betrayal and rejection by friends, and our own ongoing battles to maintain faithfulness to each other in our feelings, thoughts, and behavior. In committing ourselves to fruitfulness, we have opened ourselves to the joys and the extreme challenges of birthing 3 children in the first 4 years of our marriage.

From the day I committed my life to Jesus, not knowing what that would mean for me, to this day, I have to choose whether to live my life in light of the goodness of God, or in light of my desires for comfort, pleasure and titillation. As I face ongoing temptation, immaturity, and spiritual warfare, hope is stirred in my soul when I think about the

---

[122] Ephesians 3:19

wedding day that is coming for me; my own wedding day is only a faint shadow of that glorious day.

When we stand before Jesus and finally see His face, we won't regret one sacrifice we made to prepare ourselves for His intimacy that requires such radical commitment on our end and often feels so out of step with the world in which we live. When we see him, all questions and insecurities of what will bring us favor with people or what is politically correct will fade away — all we will care about is responding to this perfect God who has desired to have *all* of us, because He has willingly given us *all of Himself*. May we become a church who lives with this truth as our guiding thought and our True Narrative. That serves as my ongoing passion, prayer, and purpose; I pray it may become yours too.

CREATED FOR LOVE
6 WEEK TRANSFORMATIONAL STUDY AND DISCUSSION GUIDE

SESSION ONE

<u>Read</u>

Introduction and Chapter 1

<u>Discussion Questions</u>

1. Has your exposure to sexuality and desire been primarily from the church or the world? What impact do you think this has had on your beliefs and behavior?
2. Which has been your biggest tendency: to suppress sexual desire, to indulge it, or both?
3. What is an aspect of your body or gender that has been hard for you to accept?

<u>Group Ministry Exercise</u>

Take time in prayer after this discussion. Have each group member hold their desires out to God and invite God to fill those desires that have been suppressed or indulged wrongly. Make space for God to share with each group member what He says about their body and gender, particularly those aspects that have been hard for the individual to accept and bless.

SESSION TWO

<u>Read</u>

Chapters 2-3

<u>Discussion Questions</u>

1. Have the men in the group share which aspect of man's curse they see most prevalently in themselves.
2. Have the women in the group share which aspect of woman's curse they see most prevalently in themselves.

3. Have the men in the group share which aspect of woman's curse they see most prevalently in the world today, and how that affects them.

4. Have the women in the group share which aspect of man's curse they see most prevalently in the world today, and how that affects them.

5. How have you felt about "the law"? Have you seen it as oppressive, as insignificant to your life, or as a source of life?

6. Describe breakdowns you've seen in complementarity, commitment, and boundary. How have those breakdowns negatively impacted your life?

Group Ministry Exercise

After discussion, take time to sit before the Lord and allow Holy Spirit to show where each group member has fallen short of God's intentions. Cry out for mercy and help in the areas you most need it, and partner together with each other to pray and believe for Jesus to bring breakthrough.

SESSION THREE

Read

Chapters 4-5

Discussion Questions

1. What do Jesus's human interactions with those struggling with sexuality show about His character, nature, and heart?

2. How do Jesus's teachings on sexuality, marriage, and celibacy challenge you? How do they inspire you?

3. How important did the apostles treat sexuality?

4. In light of the biblical witness, where do you think you and your church's communication needs to change in order to more closely reflect a Biblical worldview and witness?

Group Ministry Exercise

Intercede as a group for the churches represented in the room. Pray for boldness, conviction, and compassion to rise. Intercede over the areas that were expressed in question 4 as areas that needed change, and ask God what role each group member is to play in that change.

SESSION FOUR

Read

Chapter 6

Discussion Questions

1. Discuss the concepts "internalization" and "detachment". What messages did you internalize growing up, and what messages or relationships did you detach from and reject?

2. What influence did your mother have on your sense of your own gender, and do you see that influence as mostly positive, negative, or both?

3. What influence did your father have on your sense of your own gender, and do you see that influence as mostly positive, negative, or both?

4. What influence did your peers have on your sense of your own gender, and do you see that influence as mostly positive, negative, or both?

5. Have you seen Jesus change your narrative or redeem broken aspects of your upbringing? If so, share how He did that and what affects you've seen from His work. If not, share a doubt, question, or belief that you'd like Him to speak into.

Group Ministry Exercise

Take time in silence to allow Holy Spirit to reveal lies you might have internalized from childhood influences. Then, allow Holy Spirit to speak into any relationships that you had walled-off or detached from. Take time before a Cross to allow Jesus to assume the pain and wounds that surface for each participant. Then, if you have time, have the group speak identity and blessing over each group member.

SESSION FIVE

<u>Read</u>

Chapters 7-8

<u>Discussion Questions</u>

1. Think about the 3 areas of transformation described: surrender, confession, and setting healthy boundaries. Which area do you feel is the most-needed growth area for you, and why?
2. Is taking authority over demons or the spiritual realm exciting, intimidating, or strange to you?
3. Share about an individual you feel called to forgive in order to release their negative affects in your development.
4. Is the expectation of a life-long process of transformation comforting or discouraging to you?
5. Which of all the "steps" on the road to wholeness do you feel you're at currently? What is Jesus's call to you right now in your process of transformation?

<u>Group Ministry Exercise</u>

Take time in group worship after this discussion. Allow Holy Spirit to minister to hope to those who are discouraged, and have those who do feel "stuck" or "discouraged" in their process receive prayer from the other group members. Practice the discipline of encouraging one another on to love and good deeds, and relish in the hope we have of eternity!

SESSION SIX

<u>Read</u>

Chapter 9 & Epilogue

<u>Discussion Questions</u>

1. Talk about a friendship that powerfully revealed the love of God in your life.
2. How would you like to grow in friendship with others?
3. Think about the different aspects of healthy sexuality: honor, Jesus-centeredness, complementarity. Which of these has been

most difficult for you?

4. What fears, walls, and disappointments come up when you think about singleness, dating or marriage?

5. Talk about a marriage in which you witnessed a good representation of the love of Christ and His Church. What about the marriage made it so vibrant?

Group Ministry Exercise

In this closing ministry time, pray a blessing over each group member. For singles, pray for their relational future, clarity, and success in friendship and dating. For married people, pray for a deeper revelation of Christ's love to flow through each of them toward one another. Bless each group member as a powerful example of the love of Jesus, and encourage each group member with the growth that you've observed in them over the last few weeks.

WITH GRATITUDE

I am indebted to many for their feedback as this book has gone through various stages of development. I first received feedback from my wonderful family, including Matt Franklin, Lou Franklin, and Matt & Allison Willis, as well as a spiritual son, Jeremiah Gentle. Andrew Comiskey took significant time talking me through important revisions that made this offering infinitely better. Through later drafts, I was blessed to receive input from Dr. Jack Tracy and Dr. Bryan Ray, who each helped me craft the psychological components with more nuance and accuracy. Jonathan Casad contributed his considerable talents regarding phrasing, grammar, and philosophy. Dr. Gary Chapman was a source of encouragement and helped me see practical ways the book could be better utilized within churches. Many thanks as well to Drew Steadman and his team at Clear Day, whose friendship, encouragement, and expertise were reliable expressions of God's care for me as writing turned toward publishing.

As always, my wife Jordyn has served as my biggest cheerleader and also a wonderful challenger to make sure I look at things from different perspectives.

BIBLIOGRAPHY

Dr. Dan B. Allender, *The Wounded Heart: Hope for Adult Victims of Childhood Sexual Abuse* (Colorado Springs: NavPress, 1990)

Stephen Black, *Freedom Realized* (Enumclaw: Redemption Press, 2017)

Andrew Comiskey, *Living Waters: Restoring Relational Integrity Through the Broken Body of Christ* (Grandview: Desert Stream Press, 2013)

Andrew Comiskey, *Naked Surrender* (Downers Grove: InterVarsity Press, 2011)

Andrew Comiskey, *Pursuing Sexual Wholeness* (Lake Mary: Charisma, 1989)

Andrew Comiskey, *Strength in Weakness: Overcoming Sexual and Relational Brokenness* (Downers Grove: InterVarsity Press, 2003)

Richard J. Foster, *Celebration of Discipline: The Path to Spiritual Growth* (New York: Harper Collins, 1988)

Richard J. Foster, *Prayer: Finding the Heart's True Home* (New York: Harper Collins, 1992)

Robert A. J. Gagnon, *The Bible and Homosexual Practice: Texts and Hermeneutics* (Nashville: Abingdon Press, 2001)

John Paul II, *Man and Woman He Created Them, A Theology of the Body*, trans. Michael Waldstein (Boston: Pauline Books, 2006)

C. S. Lewis, *The Four Loves* (Orlando: Harcourt Brace & Company, 1960)

C. S. Lewis, *Mere Christianity* (New York: Macmillan Publishing, 1978)

C. S. Lewis, *The Weight of Glory* (New York: Harper Collins, 2001)

Gerald G. May, *Addiction and Grace: Love and Spirituality in the Healing of Addictions* (New York: Harper Collins, 1988)

Geri McGhee, *Clearing the Land: Preparing for Deliverance.*

Joseph J. Nicolosi, *Shame and Attachment Loss: The Practical Work of Reparative Therapy* (Downers Grove: InterVarsity Press, 2009)

Leanne Payne, *Broken Image* (Grand Rapids: Baker Books, 1995)

Leanne Payne, *Crisis in Masculinity* (Grand Rapids: Baker Books, 1985)

Leanne Payne, *The Healing Presence: Curing the Soul through Union with Christ* (Grand Rapids: Baker Books, 1989)

Leanne Payne, *Real Presence: The Christian Worldview of C. S. Lewis as Incarnational Reality* (Grand Rapids: Baker Books, 1995)

Josef Pieper, *On Hope* (San Francisco: Ignatius Press, 1977)

Bessel Van der Kolk, *The Body Keeps the Score* (New York: Viking Penguin, 2014)

Christopher West, *Fill These Hearts* (New York: Random House, 2012)

Christopher West, *Theology of the Body Explained* (Boston: Pauline Books, 2007)

Christopher West, *Theology of the Body for Beginners: A Basic Introduction to Pope John Paul II's Sexual Revolution* (West Chester: Ascension Press, 2004)

John Wimber and Kevin Springer, *Power Healing* (New York: Harper Collins, 1987)